The IMPUTATION *of* ADAM'S SIN

by
JOHN MURRAY

PRESBYTERIAN AND REFORMED PUBLISHING CO.
Nutley, New Jersey
1977

Preface

The material presented in the pages which follow was published in four successive issues of *The Westminster Theological Journal*, XVIII, 2; XIX, 1 and 2; XX, 1. I wish to express my indebtedness to the Editor, the Rev. Professor Ned B. Stonehouse, for his generosity in accepting the articles for publication and for his care in reading and checking the manuscripts. I am likewise indebted to the Managing Editor, the Rev. Professor Paul Woolley, for his labour and care in correcting the proofs. To the Board of Trustees of Westminster Theological Seminary I extend my warm thanks for a leave of absence during 1955 and 1956. It was the leisure granted from other duties during that period that enabled me to undertake some of the research required for the writing of this study.

Grateful acknowledgment is hereby extended to the following publishers for permission to quote from copyrighted books: the Muhlenberg Press, Philadelphia, from Anders Nygren: *Commentary on Romans* (1949); the Lutterworth Press, London, from Emil Brunner: *The Christian Doctrine of Creation and Redemption, Dogmatics* II (1952); the B. Herder Book Co., St. Louis, from H. J. Schroeder: *Canons and Decrees of the Council of Trent* (1941) and from Joseph Pohle, ed. Arthur Preuss: *God the Author of Nature and the Supernatural* (1934); The Macmillan Co., New York, from George D. Smith, ed.: *The Teaching of the Catholic Church* (1949).

I wish to express my deep gratitude to the Wm. B. Eerdmans Publishing Company for undertaking to publish these articles in book form.

JOHN MURRAY

CONTENTS

CHAPTER ONE

THEOLOGICAL thought of the present day is not only hospitable to the notion of solidarity in sin and guilt; it is keenly sensitive to the fact of such solidarity. Dealing with the Augustinian doctrine of original sin, Emil Brunner can say: "I want to make it clear from the outset that I am in complete agreement with the twofold aim of Augustine: to represent sin as a dominant force, and humanity as bound together in a solidarity of guilt".[1] And C. H. Dodd, commenting on Paul's argument in Romans 5:12–21, says: "What lies behind it is the ancient conception of solidarity. The moral unit was the community . . . rather than the individual . . . . Thus the whole of humanity could be thought of as the tribe of Adam, and Adam's sin was the sin of the race. With the growing appreciation of the ethical significance of the individual, the old idea of solidarity weakened. But it corresponded with real facts. The isolation of the individual is an abstraction."[2] "Adam", he continues, "is a name which stands to him (Paul) for the 'corporate personality' of mankind."[3] Yet of Romans 5:12 Brunner also says: "It does not refer to the transgression of Adam in which all his descendants share; but it states the fact that 'Adam's' descendants are involved in death, because they themselves commit sin".[4] And C. H. Dodd can also say: "Thus Paul's doctrine of Christ as the 'second Adam' is not so bound up with the story of the Fall as a literal happening that it ceases to have meaning when we no longer accept the story as such. Indeed, we should not too readily assume that Paul did so accept it."[5] We thus

---

[1] *The Christian Doctrine of Creation and Redemption. Dogmatics*, Vol. II (London, 1952), p. 103.
[2] *The Epistle of Paul to the Romans* (London, 1934), p. 79.
[3] *Ibid.*, p. 80.
[4] *Op. cit.*, p. 104.
[5] *Op. cit.*, p. 80.

5

see that the recognition of and the emphasis upon solidaric or corporate sin and guilt in our present-day theology are not to be interpreted as identical with the classic protestant doctrine of the imputation of Adam's sin. And it does not advance the cause of theology or of exegesis to regard Paul's appeal to the fall of Adam as but the mythical form in which the fact of solidaric unity in sin is expressed. It is not a work of supererogation, therefore, if we address ourselves anew to this question of the imputation of Adam's sin to posterity and to the study of the passage upon which, more than any other, the doctrine is based. It is encouraging to find in so brilliant a scholar as Anders Nygren so appreciative an assessment of the pivotal place which Romans 5:12–19 occupies in this major epistle. "The parallelism which Paul draws between Adam and Christ has seemed so strange and unmanageable that it has made scholars the more willing to treat this section as a parenthesis. More or less consciously interpreters have acted on the assumption that something, which is so foreign to today's thought as to seem unreal, cannot have been of decisive importance to Paul either. To explain how he happened in on the digression, reference has, for instance, been made to the important place which the 'Adam-speculation' came to play in rabbinical thought.... We should not forget that Paul read about Adam on one of the first pages of his Bible; so it is not necessary to look for remoter sources from which the idea might have come.... Paul does not look on Christ as an Adam redivivus. He sets up Adam and Christ in this parallel, not to affirm their identity, but contrariwise to point out the contrast between them. When once one comes to realize what that means to Paul, he forthwith discovers that this passage is by no means a parenthesis or a digression in the apostle's thought. Rather do we here come to the high point of the epistle. This is the point where all the lines of his thinking converge, both those of the preceding chapters and those of the chapters that follow."[6]

In studying Romans 5:12–19 as it bears upon the question of the imputation of Adam's sin to posterity we shall subsume

[6] Anders Nygren: *Commentary on Romans* (Philadelphia, 1949), pp. 207–209.

our discussion under the following main subdivisions: I Syntactical Construction; II The Sin Contemplated; III The Union Involved; IV The Nature of the Imputation; V The Sin Imputed.

I. SYNTACTICAL CONSTRUCTION

It is scarcely necessary to argue the fact that verse 12 is an unfinished comparison. Few interpreters dispute this fact. καὶ οὕτως in the middle of the verse does not have the effect of closing the comparison introduced by ὥσπερ. In that event we should have οὕτως καὶ and not καὶ οὕτως (cf. vss. 15, 18, 19, 21 and 6:4, 11). καὶ οὕτως is coordinative or continuative and does not mean "even so" but rather "and so" or "and in like manner" (cf. Acts 7:8; 28:14; I Cor. 7:17, 36; 11:28; Gal. 6:2). Even Pelagius did not suppose anything different as far as the syntax of verse 12 was concerned. The Latin text on which he based his comments was faithful to the Greek in this particular — et ita in omnes homines [mors] pertransiit.[7]

It is not difficult to discover the reason why the comparison introduced in verse 12 had been broken off. The development of Paul's thought required a parenthesis after the concluding clause of verse 12. This parenthesis begins at verse 13 and continues through verse 17. It may well be that we should not regard these five verses as one parenthesis but as two, the first consisting of verses 13 and 14 and the second of verses 15–17. On this construction of the parenthetical portion we should have to say that the thought expressed in verse 12, especially in the last clause, dictated the necessity of appending without delay the data expressed in verses 13 and 14, and then, in turn, the typological datum enunciated at the end of verse 14 — "who is the type of the one to come" — necessitated the setting forth of the series of similitudes, but particularly of contrasts, instituted in verses 15–17.[8] However

---

[7] See *Pelagius's Expositions of Thirteen Epistles of St. Paul*, ed. Alexander Souter (Cambridge, 1926), No. 2, p. 45 in *Texts and Studies. Contributions to Biblical and Patristic Literature*, ed. J. Armitage Robinson, Vol. IX, No. 2.

[8] *Cf.* Heinrich A. W. Meyer: *Critical and Exegetical Handbook to the Epistle to the Romans* (E. T., New York, 1884), pp. 193 f. "The illustration,

we construe these five verses, as one parenthesis or as two, it is quite apparent that Paul does not return to the type of syntax which had been begun in verse 12, but had been broken off, until we arrive at verse 18. Here we have a finished comparison with both protasis and apodosis, the former intimated in ὡς and the latter in οὕτως καί. "Consequently then, as through one trespass judgment came upon all men unto condemnation, even so through one righteous act judgment came upon all men unto justification of life."

It is not of much consequence to determine whether verse 18 is resumptive or recapitulatory.[9] It is sufficient for us to know that Paul does not leave us in any doubt as to what the apodosis of verse 12 would have been if it had been completed in terms of the protasis which verse 12 supplies. The completed comparisons of verses 18, 19 place beyond all doubt what the governing thought of this passage is and it is in terms of that governing thought that the comparison of verse 12 would have to be completed.

This parenthesis of verses 13–17, which at first seems to be so awkward and perplexing, proves on closer examination to be eloquent in determining for us the precise import of the clause which, after all, is the most crucial in the exegesis of this whole passage, namely, the last clause in verse 12. The interpretation is established by the eloquent repetitions of the succeeding verses and, as we shall have occasion to note, no consideration is more pertinent to the question than the fact that verses 13–17 are in the form of a parenthesis.

---

namely, introduced in vv. 13, 14 of the ἐφ' ᾧ πάντες ἥμαρτον now rendered it impossible to add the second half of the comparison *syntactically* belonging to the ὥσπερ, and therefore the Apostle, driven on by the rushing flow of ideas to this point, from which he can no longer revert to the construction with which he started, has no hesitation in dropping the latter . . . and in subsequently bringing in *merely* the main tenor of what is wanting by the relative clause attached to 'Αδάμ: ὅς ἐστι τύπος τοῦ μέλλοντος in ver. 14."

[9] Meyer (*ibid.*, p. 194; *cf.* p. 215) argues against other interpreters who hold that in verse 18 the first half of the comparison is resumed and urges in support of his view "not only the unprecedented length, but still more the contents of the supposed parenthesis, which in fact already comprehends in itself the parallel under every aspect" and he concludes: "In ver. 18 f. we have *recapitulation*, but not *resumption*".

II. The Sin Contemplated

The crux of the question in connection with this passage is the reference in the clause ἐφ' ᾧ πάντες ἥμαρτον in verse 12. This clause informs us why death passed on to all men and should be rendered "in that all sinned".[10] Hence the question is: to what does Paul refer when he says "all sinned"? As far as form is concerned the expression itself could refer to the actual sins of men (cf. Romans 3:23). Furthermore, if Paul meant the actual sins of all men, this is without doubt the expression he would have used; no other would have been more suitable to express that thought. The meaning, however, is not to be determined by grammatical possibility but by contextual considerations. There are various views of the force of this expression.

1. The Pelagian view.

This view is that the clause in question refers to the actual sins of men.[11] In this event the thought of Paul would be that as Adam sinned and therefore died so in like manner all men

---

[10] It is unnecessary at this stage in the history of exposition to argue that the Vulgate rendering, in quo omnes peccaverunt, though, as we shall see, it is theologically true, is nevertheless grammatically untenable. The force of ἐφ' ᾧ is causal and it means "in that", "by the fact that", or simply "because".

[11] Cf. Pelagius: op. cit. "Propter ea sicut per unum hominem in hunc mundum peccatum intróiit et per peccatum mors. Exemplo uel forma. quo modo, cum non esset peccatum, per Adam aduenit, ita etiam, cum paene aput nullum iustitia remansisset, per Christum est reuocata . . . Et ita in omnes homines [mors] pertransiit, in quo omnes peccauerunt. Dum ita peccant, et similiter moriuntur" (p. 45). "Sicut enim per inoboedientiam unius hominis peccatoris constituti sunt plurimi, ita et per unius oboedientiam iusti constituentur multi. Sicut exemplo inoboedientiae Adae peccauerunt multi, ita et Christi oboedientia justificantur multi" (p. 48).

Cf. also Edouard Reuss: La Bible: Traduction Nouvelle avec Introductions et Commentaires (Paris, 1898) ad Romans 5:12–14. "Tous les hommes issus d'Adam péchèrent également. . . . Il n'y a pas un mot dans le texte qui puisse servir à étayer les thèses scolastiques d'un changement opéré dans la nature de l'homme, de la nécessité de pécher, de l'imputation du péché de tous. Mais il tient aussi a le prouver. Comment le prouve-t-il? Par un autre fait également général et tout à fait incontestable. C'est que tous les hommes issus d'Adam sont morts." Emil Brunner (op. cit., p. 99),

die because they sin. Adam is the prototype — he sinned and brought sin and death into the world. Others in like manner sin and they also are afflicted with death. The coordination of sin and death, exemplified in Adam, applies in every case where there is sin.

It needs to be observed that the construction of verse 12 does not disprove this interpretation. Even though on this view we should have expected Paul to use οὕτως καί at the middle of the verse rather than καὶ οὕτως, yet it is possible to think of Paul as enunciating the parallelism between the entrance of sin and death through Adam and the passing on of sin and death through all without closing the comparison in terms of the analogy that obtains in the opposite sphere of righteousness and life. In other words, the syntax of verse 12 cannot of itself be pleaded as a conclusive argument against the Pelagian view. There are, however, conclusive objections on factual, exegetical, and theological grounds.

(i) The Pelagian view is not actually or historically true. Not all die because they actually and voluntarily sin. Infants die. But they have not actually transgressed after the similitude of Adam's transgression.

(ii) In verses 13, 14 Paul states the opposite of the Pelagian view. For here we are told that death reigned over those who did not sin after the similitude of Adam's transgression. What or whom Paul has in view is difficult to determine, but it is obvious that he is thinking of death as exercising its sway over persons who did not sin as Adam did. It is futile to try to evade the direct bearing of this fact upon the Pelagian interpretation. Paul is saying the opposite, namely, that death reigns universally and therefore reigns over those who are in a different category from that of Adam.[12]

while right in recognising that *in quo omnes peccaverunt* is a mis-translation, puts himself in the Pelagian category as far as interpretation of this text is concerned when he says that "these words mean the exact opposite: namely, that each of us becomes a sinner by his own act".

[12] This consideration that not all men are in the category of Adam militates against Brunner's conception that we are all "Adam". For if we all are "Adam" in respect of Paul's teaching in this passage, then how can Paul speak of some as not sinning after the similitude of Adam's transgression? In other words, in terms of the datum which is the pivotal

(iii) The most conclusive refutation of the Pelagian interpretation is derived from the repeated and emphatic affirmations of Paul in the immediate context, affirmations to the
effect that the universal sway of condemnation and death is
to be referred to the *one sin* of the *one man* Adam. On at least
five occasions in verses 15–19 this principle is asserted — "by
the trespass of the one the many died" (vs. 15); "the judgment was from one unto condemnation" (vs. 16); "by the
trespass of the one death reigned through the one" (vs. 17);
"through one trespass judgment came upon all men unto
condemnation" (vs. 18); "through the disobedience of the one
man the many were constituted sinners" (vs. 19). We might
think that Paul has needlessly repeated himself, but it is a
repetition which establishes beyond dispute that Paul regards
condemnation and death as having passed on to all men by
the one trespass of the one man Adam. It is quite impossible
to construe this emphasis upon the one sin of the one man as
equivalent to the actual personal sin of countless individuals.
It is indisputable, therefore, that Paul regards the universality
of condemnation and death as grounded upon and proceeding
from the one trespass of the one man Adam.   And the
Pelagian insistence that death and condemnation find their
ground solely in the personal voluntary sin of the individuals
of the race cannot be harmonised with this sustained witness
of the apostle.

(iv) The Pelagian exegesis destroys the force of the analogy
which Paul institutes in this passage as a whole. The doctrine
Paul is illustrating by appeal to the analogy of the condemnation and death proceeding from Adam is the doctrine that men
are justified by the free grace of God on the basis of the
righteousness and obedience of Christ. What Paul has been
controverting in the earlier part of the epistle is that men are
justified by their own works. He is establishing the truth that
men are justified and attain to life by what another has done,
the one man Jesus Christ. How vacuous and contradictory

one in the analogy which Paul is using, namely, the one trespass of the one
man Adam, we are not all "Adam". It is to waive exegesis altogether if we
do not take account of the uniqueness, the "oneness" of Adam in respect
of the position he occupies in this passage.

would be any appeal to the parallel obtaining in the relation of Adam to the race if the Pelagian construction were that of Paul, namely, that men die simply because of their own sin and not at all on the ground of Adam's sin! Paul's doctrine of justification would be nullified if, at this point, the parallel he uses to illustrate and confirm it is after the pattern of the Pelagian construction. For it would mean that men are justified by their own voluntary action just as they come under condemnation solely by their own voluntary sin. This is indeed Pelagian doctrine but that it contradicts the teaching of Paul lies on the face of the epistle. The doctrine of justification which this epistle establishes is a doctrine which cannot tolerate as its analogy or parallel a construction of the reign of sin, condemnation, and death which bears any resemblance to the Pelagian. Hence the Pelagian view must be rejected on this ground as well as on that of the others mentioned.

2. *The Roman Catholic View.*

It cannot be maintained that there has been unanimity among Roman Catholic theologians respecting Romans 5:12 or about the clause with which we are more particularly concerned. At the time of the Council of Trent Ambrosius Catharinus held a position similar to that which we shall later on propound as the correct view. He maintained that the sin referred to in the clause, "in that all sinned", is the actual voluntary transgression of Adam imputed to all posterity by reason of the covenant relationship which Adam sustained to the race — when Adam sinned all mankind sinned with him and in him. He insisted that the sin of every one is the act only of the transgression of Adam and not the privation of righteousness or the concupiscence which were the consequences of that sin. It is this sin of Adam imputed to posterity that Catharinus called "original sin" and it is that sin and that alone, he contended, that Paul has in view in Romans 5:12–19.[13] Albertus Pighius, a contemporary of Catharinus held the same position. He is explicit to the effect that the apostle constantly refers the reign of death and the judgment

---

[13] For Catharinus' view see Pietro Soaue Polano: *The Historie of the Councel of Trent* (E. T. by Nathanael Brent, London, 1640), pp. 175 ff.

of condemnation, under which we all are concluded, to the one sin of the one man Adam. In him, therefore, not in us, was that sin by which we all have sinned. Even infants are guilty and constituted sinners not on account of their own sin but on account of the sin and disobedience of Adam.[14]

This position is not, however, the official teaching of the Romish Church, and her theologians have followed a different line of thought. The Council of Trent in its "Decretum de Peccato Originali" says: "1. If anyone does not confess that the first man, Adam, when he transgressed the commandment of God in paradise, immediately lost the holiness and justice in which he had been constituted, and through the offense of that prevarication incurred the wrath and indignation of God, and thus death with which God had previously threatened him, and, together with death, captivity under his power who thenceforth *had the empire of death, that is to say, the devil*, and that the entire Adam through that offense of prevarication was changed in body and soul for the worse, let him be anathema.

"2. If anyone asserts that the transgression of Adam injured him alone and not his posterity, and that the holiness and justice which he received from God, which he lost, he lost for himself alone and not for us also; or that he, being defiled by the sin of disobedience, has transfused only death and the pains of the body into the whole human race, but not sin also, which is the death of the soul, let him be anathema."[15] One

[14] See Albertus Pighius: *Controversiarum Praecipuarum . . . Luculenta Explicatio* (Cologne, 1542). In dealing with Rom. 5:12–19 he says: "Uides, ut Apostolus perpetuo, et constantissime uni peccato unius Adae, acceptum referat mortis regnum, et damnationis, sub quo omnes conclusi sumus, iudicium: unufn, et unius peccatum dicit, cuius demerito, omnes mortui sumus . . . . In illo, non in nobis, peccasse omnes. In illo ergo, non in nobis fuit illud peccatum, quo peccauimus omnes. Unius illius inobedientia, non sua propria, peccatores constitutos multos, qui per aetatem, sub lege nondum existentes, sua inobedientia potuerunt peccatores fieri . . . . Proinde, quasi interrogares, ob cuius peccatum paruulus, reus, et peccator sit, tibi diserte respondet Apostolus, non ob suum, sed ob Adae peccatum, illum reatu constringi, et peccatorem constitui . . ." (Fol. XXIV a). *Cf.* for a succinct statement of Pighius' position Martin Chemnitz: *Examen Concilii Tridentini* (Berlin, 1861), p. 103.

[15] As translated by H. J. Schroeder: *Canons and Decrees of the Council of Trent* (St. Louis and London, 1941), p. 21.

would gather from these statements that the sin of Adam which is the sin of all is that which by propagation is transfused into all. Obviously this notion is quite distinct from that of the imputation to all of the actual transgression of Adam, as espoused by Catharinus and Pighius.

It is this direction of thought, which appears in the decrees of Trent, that has been characteristic of Romish theologians in the formulation of this doctrine. It is not that Rome in any way denies the fact or the consequences of the actual transgression of Adam. It is simply that in the interpretation of Romans 5:12 and of the sin in which all are implicated by reason of the sin of Adam this sin is conceived of not as the actual sin of Adam imputed but as the habitual sin that is conveyed by natural generation. The matter is stated clearly by Joseph Pohle: "The sin of Adam is original in a twofold sense: (1) As a sinful personal act (*peccatum originale originans*), and (2) as a sinful state (*peccatum originale originatum*). It is the state not the act that is transmitted to Adam's descendants."[16] There are two respects in which the former bears upon the latter. First, the sinful personal act brought the sinful state into existence and, second, the sinful state is truly sinful "only in its logical connexion with Adam's voluntary transgression of the divine command in Paradise".[17] But it is only "the habitual sin of Adam (*habitus peccati*), which 'entered into this world' through him, i. e., was by him transmitted to all his progeny".[18]

Rome is reluctant to define precisely that in which this original and habitual sin consists. Insofar as definition is ventured it is conceived of as consisting chiefly in the privation of holiness and justice.[19] But since man's fall also entailed the loss of integrity, it is hard for Romish theologians to exclude concupiscence from the ambit of original sin. Hence while they

---

[16] Joseph Pohle, ed. Arthur Preuss: *God the Author of Nature and the Supernatural* (St. Louis and London, 1934), p. 233.

[17] *Ibid.*, p. 246.

[18] *Ibid.*, p. 248.

[19] "Original sin essentially consists in privation of grace, so far as this is voluntary in all men through the will of their progenitor" (*ibid.*, p. 269). *Cf.* also ed. George D. Smith: *The Teaching of the Catholic Church* (New York, 1949), Vol. I, p. 345.

are emphatic in maintaining that original sin does not consist in concupiscence,[20] nevertheless they are willing to grant that concupiscence, though it is not itself truly and properly sin, is embraced in the ambit of habitual sin.[21]

After taking all these distinctions and qualifications into account the upshot is that in Romish theology the sin referred to in the last clause of Romans 5:12 is the habitual or original sin which is transmitted to or transfused into Adam's posterity by natural generation and which as to its nature consists essentially in the privation of sanctity, a privation which can be categorised as sinful because of the logical relation it sustains to the voluntary transgression of Adam.[22] In a word, the sin of Romans 5:12 on account of which death passed on to all is transmitted sinfulness.

It is not our interest at the present time to examine the Romish doctrine of original sin. On this question the battle of the Reformation was closely joined and it would appear that the situation as it exists today does not offer any reason for the abatement of that controversy. But our question at present is not whether Rome's doctrine of original sin is correct but whether it is the notion of *original sin* as distinguished from *imputed sin* that Paul has in mind when he says, "in that all sinned". As far as this question is concerned we are examining the tenability of the interpretation entertained by some protestants as well as that of Rome. There are decisive objections of an exegetical and theological character to this interpretation.

(i) There is, first of all, a presumptive argument. It would

[20] "Concupiscence as such does not constitute the essence of original sin" (*ibid.*, p. 261).

[21] *Cf.* Ad. Tanquerey: *Synopsis Theologiae Dogmaticae* (New York, 1933), Tom. II, p. 566. "Ergo peccatum de quo agit S. Paulus non est peccatum actuale; nec aliunde mera poenalitas aut sola concupiscentia, sed peccatum *sui generis*, peccatum *habituale* quod in suo ambitu complectitur *reatum culpae, concupiscentiam* seu inclinationem ad peccandum, et utriusque *transmissionem* in omnes homines ob solius Adae culpam."

[22] "Thus original sin, as it is in each one of us, is voluntary, not indeed by any act of our personal will, but through the act of the 'family will,' through our relationship of spiritual dependence upon and solidarity with our first, divinely appointed, supernatural head and representative Adam" (Geo. D. Smith: *op. cit.*, p. 348).

be exceedingly difficult to adjust the notion in question to the thought expressed by the aorist ἥμαρτον. Original sin as construed by Rome or, for that matter, by protestants is that which is being constantly conveyed by natural generation. As respects conveyance there is a constant process and as respects result there is a constant condition. If the sin alluded to in the clause concerned is original sin, then both the process and the condition are in view as defining the sin. How an historical or indefinite aorist could be used to denote such a sin it is difficult, if not impossible, to conceive. About the only way in which the aorist could be used is by focusing attention on the historical inception of this process and condition. But the Romish interpretation does not thus limit the thought and if original sin is meant it would not be feasible to limit the thought to the once-for-all historical inception. The more we think of this objection the more cogent it becomes. But we are willing to characterise it as presumptive rather than conclusive.

(ii) More cogent is the theological consideration that this view does not accord with the parallel or analogy which Paul institutes in this passage. The validity of this argument rests, of course, upon the outright rejection of the Romish view of justification. Rome regards justification as consisting in regeneration and renovation wrought by the infusion of righteousness and her theologians in dealing with Romans 5:12–19 appeal to this concept of justification in support of their interpretation of verse 12, to wit, that there is an obvious parallel between the infusion of righteousness in justification and the transfusion of original sin on account of the sin of Adam. We cannot now digress to refute this doctrine of justification. We must be content with the assertion that it is flatly contradictory of the biblical and Pauline teaching. The doctrine of Paul is that we are justified on the basis of the righteousness of Christ and not by a righteousness infused into us any more than by a righteousness wrought by us. Since this is Paul's doctrine and since he institutes a parallel between the way in which condemnation and death pass on to all men and the way in which justification and life pass on to the justified, the *modus operandi* in the latter case cannot find its analogue in the transfusion or transmission of original sin. The parallel which Paul's doctrine of justification demands must be of a very different sort. So, in brief, the requirements of the analogy instituted are not fulfilled but rather violated by importing into Paul's thought in this passage the notion of transmitted and inherited sin.

(iii) Most conclusive is the objection that the interpretation being debated is inconsistent with the repeated affirmations of Paul in Romans 5:15–19. We have had occasion to refer to these in the refutation of the Pelagian view. But it is well to be reminded that Paul on at least five occasions in successive verses (15, 16, 17, 18, 19) refers the universal reign of condemnation and death to the one trespass of the one man Adam. This sustained emphasis upon the "oneness" of the sin and of the man does not comport with the notion of original sin. Though the Romanist view recognises that original sin proceeds from the actual transgression of Adam, yet original sin, as that which is transmitted or transfused, is the sin that belongs to all who come by natural generation and cannot be regarded as conforming to such a specification as the one sin of the one man Adam. What is with us habitual, as the Romanist theologians assert, can scarcely be characterised as the one trespass of Adam.

For these reasons we shall have to reject this interpretation of the clause, "in that all sinned".

3. Calvin's Interpretation.

Calvin's view of original sin is radically different from that of Rome. According to Calvin the original sin which is conveyed by natural generation is itself, intrinsically, radical depravity. The protestant polemic was directed with vigour against the Romish view that original sin consisted simply in the privation of original righteousness and integrity and that the concupiscence which resulted from the loss of integrity was not itself truly and properly sinful, and the Romish polemic was directed with equal vigour against the protestant doctrine that original sin involved a radical corruption of our moral and spiritual nature. The respective polemics of these two branches of Christendom must be understood in this light and any agreement there may be respecting the relation of Adam's actual transgression to the original sin with which all are inflicted must not obscure the difference on the nature of original sin itself.

But though Calvin's view of original sin differs so radically from that of Rome his view of the crucial clause in Romans 5:12, "in that all sinned", is, exegetically speaking, similar to that of Rome. For he, in like manner, regards Paul as referring here to original sin. "But Paul distinctly affirms that sin is propagated to all who suffer its punishment. And this he afterwards more expressly declares when a little later he assigns the reason why all of Adam's posterity are subject to the dominion of death, even this, he says, seeing that we all have sinned (quoniam omnes peccavimus). But to sin is in this case to be corrupt and vitiated. For that natural depravity which we bring from our mother's womb, though it does not immediately bring forth its fruits, is nevertheless sin in the sight of God and deserves his vengeance. And this is the sin which they call original. For so Adam at his first creation received both for himself and for posterity the gifts of divine favour, so by falling away from the Lord he in himself corrupted, vitiated, depraved, and ruined our nature. Having been divested of God's likeness he could not have begotten seed but like himself. Therefore we all have sinned because we have all been imbued with natural corruption, and so are become wicked and perverse."[23]

The same objections apply to this interpretation as apply to the Romanist position. While it is true that Calvin is not encumbered by the difficulty Romish exegetes encounter when they are faced with the necessity of categorising as sinful that which does not intrinsically meet the requirements of their own definition of sin and while Calvin's view of original sin is thoroughly Pauline and biblical, yet, exegetically, he has not been successful in analysing the precise thought of the apostle in this passage. In other words, he has not been able to get above the Augustinian tradition in the exposition of Romans 5:12.

---

[23] *Comm. ad* Rom. 5:12; *cf. ad* Rom. 5:15, 17.

4. *The Classic Protestant Interpretation.*

The pivotal question is still before us: what sin does Paul have in view when he says, "in that all sinned"? In order to arrive at what we believe to be the proper view it is necessary to take account of the following considerations.

(i) It is unquestionable that the universal sway of death is represented in verse 12 as resting upon the fact that "all sinned". Whatever the sin contemplated may be, it is the reason why death passed through to all men. And this is simply to say that it is the ground of the universality of death.

(ii) In verses 15–19, however, Paul with unmistakeable clearness asserts that the universal reign of death rests upon the one trespass of the one man Adam. "By the trespass of the one the many died" (vs. 15); "By the trespass of the one death reigned through the one" (vs. 17). And, of course, this relationship in reference to death is coordinate with and parallel to Paul's other statements in reference to condemnation. "The judgment was from one unto condemnation" (vs. 16); "Through one trespass judgment came upon all men unto condemnation" (vs. 18). Death and condemnation reign over all because of the one trespass of Adam.

(iii) Are we to suppose that Paul is dealing with two different facts when in verse 12 he grounds the death of all in the sin of all and when in verses 15 and 17 he grounds that same death in the one trespass of Adam? Are we to think that in verse 12 Paul is speaking of the sin which is personally and distributively universal either as action or as *habitus* whereas in verses 15–19 he is speaking of sin in its specific singularity as the one trespass of the one man Adam? The conclusion to which the exegetical considerations drive us is that this cannot be the case but rather that Paul must have in view the same sin when in verse 12 he says "all sinned" and when in verses 15–19 he refers to the one sin of the one man. The arguments establishing this conclusion are as follows.

(a) The whole passage (Rom. 5:12–19) is a unit. We cannot fail to see that the central structure is the analogy that obtains between the *modus operandi* of sin, condemnation, death, on the one hand, and of righteousness, justification, life, on the other. In the nature of the case, since the latter complex is for the purpose of negating the first, there are significant and magnificent contrasts, and on these Paul elaborates. But the central strand is the parallelism, and even the contrasts are based upon this substructure. Since this is the case we are forced to conclude that the comparison introduced in verse 12, though broken off and not completed in the express terms which the protasis of verse 12 would suggest and dictate, is in essential thought identical with that which is stated in its completeness in verses 18 and 19. This means that the sin referred to in verse 12, particularly in the last clause, must be that same sin that is defined in verse 18 as "the one trespass" and in verse 19 as "the disobedience of the one man". And when we go back to the three preceding verses (15–17) and bear in mind the closely knit unity of the passage, we must conclude that the same sin is in view in verses 15, 17 where it is called the trespass of the one..

(b) Verse 12 is an unfinished comparison. We only know of its implied apodosis from the following verses. It would be impossible to suppose that Paul, dealing expressly with the subject of the universal reign of death, should so explicitly and repeatedly affirm in the succeeding verses something quite different from that which he affirms in what is the unfinished introduction of his argument. If verse 12 were in a context of its own and if there were some plausible evidence of transition from one phase of teaching to another, then we could say that in verse 12 he deals with one fact and in verses 15–19 with another. But the fact that verse 12 does not complete the comparison and relies upon the succeeding verses to supply this completion makes it totally impossible to posit any transition from one phase of truth to another.

(c) As far as actual personal sin is concerned verse 14 excludes the possibility of interpreting the last clause of verse 12 in such terms. Verse 12 tells us the reason why death passed on to all men. It is that "all sinned". But verse 14 tells us that death reigned over those who did not sin after the similitude of Adam's transgression. The reign of death in verse 14 must have the same import as the passing on of death in verse 12. Hence Paul is saying that death passed on to and reigned over those who did not personally and voluntarily transgress as Adam did, and therefore the "all sinned" of verse 12 cannot refer to individual personal transgression.

For these reasons we are compelled to infer that when Paul says "all sinned" (vs. 12) and when he speaks of the one trespass of the one man (vss. 15–19) he must be referring to the same fact or event, that the one event or fact can be expressed in terms of both singularity and universality. If this identity confronts us, how are we to explain it? How can Paul say that "all sinned" and then that one sinned and refer to the same fact?

As we attempt to answer this question there is one error we must avoid. We must not tone down the singularity or the universality. Paul's language is eloquent of both. The only solution is that there must be some kind of solidarity existing between the "one" and the "all" with the result that the sin contemplated can be regarded at the same time and with equal relevance as the sin of the "one" or as the sin of "all". What this solidarity is is the subject of the next main subdivision of our discussion.

CHAPTER TWO

III. The Union Involved

THE principle of solidarity is embedded in the Scripture and is exemplified in numerous ways. It is not necessary to enumerate the instances in which the principle comes to expression. It is a patent fact that in God's government of men there are the institutions of the family, of the state, and of the church in which solidaric or corporate relationships obtain and are operative. This is simply to say that God's relations to men and the relations of men to one another are not exclusively individualistic; God deals with men in terms of these corporate relationships and men must reckon with their corporate relations and responsibilities.

There is also the institution of the individual, and to discount our individuality is to desecrate our responsible relations to God and to men. The principle of solidarity can be exaggerated; it can become an obsession and lead to fatalistic abuse (*cf.* Ezek. 18:2). All such exaggeration is evil. But it is also evil to conceive of our relations to God and to men atomistically so that we fail to appreciate the corporate entities which to such a large extent condition our life and responsibility. Solidarity works for good and for evil. It is scarcely necessary to be reminded of the beneficent influences which have emanated from its application in the realm of grace. Redemption in its design, accomplishment, application, and consummation is fashioned in terms of this principle. And in the realm of evil it is a fact of revelation and of observation that God visits "the iniquity of the fathers upon the children unto the third and fourth generation of them that hate" him (Exod. 20:5).

It is consonant with these facts of the biblical revelation and of our human experience that the principle of solidarity should come to its broadest and most inclusive expression in racial solidarity and we should not be surprised to find in this case the prototypal solidarity. Racial solidarity is the only possible construction of the various data which the Scripture brings to our attention. Paul bears pointed witness to this fact when he says that "in Adam all die" (I Cor. 15:22). And it is this same solidaric relationship that forms the background of his thought when he says, "The first man Adam was made a living soul; the last Adam was made a life-giving Spirit" (I Cor. 15:45).

If we appreciate this fact of racial solidarity and therefore the solidaric relationship which Adam sustains to posterity and posterity to him, we shall be less reluctant, to say the least, to entertain the proposition that the one trespass of Adam can properly be construed as the sin of all.

The fact of solidarity does not, however, determine for us the question of its nature. What is the nature of the union that existed between Adam and posterity? On any biblically oriented view of Adam, it will be granted that from Adam proceeded by way of natural generation all the other members of the human race, that Adam was the natural father of all mankind. It might appear to be an adequate answer to our question to say that the union between Adam and posterity is biological and genealogical and that no more is required to explain the facts. This is to say that Adam was the "natural root" of all mankind. Levi was in the loins of his father Abraham when the latter paid tithes to Melchizedek, and thus it can be said that Levi paid tithes to Melchizedek (Heb. 7:9, 10). In like manner all were in the loins of Adam when he sinned, and so it can be said that they sinned in him and fell with him in his first transgression. It may not be alleged that the fact of seminal relationship is irrelevant in this connection. We may not presume to say that the solidarity of the race with Adam, by reason of which all are involved in his sin, could have been true if he had not been the father of all mankind. Whatever additional principle of solidarity may be posited or established it cannot be abstracted from the fact of biological ancestry.

Exegetes and theologians have not been content to explain the solidarity with Adam in terms simply of our lineage from him. They have been constrained to posit some solidaric relationship other than the genealogical as necessary to a proper grounding of the involvement in Adam's sin, whether this additional relationship is conceived of as coordinate with the genealogical or as in itself the specific ground of the imputation of Adam's first sin. There are two views of this relationship that are worthy of serious consideration. And perhaps they are the only views that can worthily claim consideration. The one is that human nature was numerically and specifically one in Adam and the other that Adam was the appointed head and representative of the whole race.

1. *The Realistic View*

Perhaps the ablest exponent and defender of the view that human nature was both numerically and specifically one in Adam is William G. T. Shedd. "The doctrine of the specific unity of Adam and his posterity", he says, "removes the great difficulties connected with the imputation of Adam's sin to his posterity, that arise from the injustice of punishing a person for a sin in which he had no kind of participation."[24] And in controverting the representative view he says: "To impute Adam's first sin to his posterity merely, and only, because Adam sinned as a representative in their room and place, makes the imputation an arbitrary act of sovereignty, not a righteous judicial act which carries in it an intrinsic morality and justice".[25]

In brief, the position is that human nature in its unindividualized unity existed in its entirety in Adam, that, when Adam sinned, not only did he sin but also the common nature which existed in its unity in him, and that, since each person who comes into the world is an individualization of this one human nature, each person as an "individualized portion" of that common nature is both culpable and punishable for the sin committed by that unity.[26] "This unity commits the first

[24] William G. T. Shedd: *Dogmatic Theology* (New York, 1889), Vol. II, p. 30.
[25] *Ibid.*, p. 36.
[26] *Cf. ibid.*, pp. 43 f.

sin. . . . This sin is imputed to the unity that committed it, inheres in the unity, and is propagated out of the unity. Consequently, all the particulars regarding sin that apply to the unity or common nature apply equally and strictly to each individualized portion of it. The individual Socrates was a fractional part of the human nature that 'sinned in, and fell with Adam in his first transgression'. . . . Consequently, the commission, imputation, inherence, and propagation of original sin cleave indissolubly to the individualized part of the common nature, as they did to the unindividualized whole of it. The distribution and propagation of the nature make no alteration in it, except in respect to *form*."[27]

To much the same effect is the view of A. H. Strong. Calling it the Augustinian theory, he says: "It holds that God imputes the sin of Adam immediately to all his posterity, in virtue of that organic unity of mankind by which the whole race at the time of Adam's transgression existed, not individually, but seminally, in him as its head. The total life of humanity was then in Adam; the race as yet had its being only in him. Its essence was not yet individualized; its forces were not yet distributed; the powers which now exist in separate men were then unified and localized in Adam; Adam's will was yet the will of the species. In Adam's free act, the will of the race revolted from God and the nature of the race corrupted itself. . . . Adam's sin is imputed to us immediately, therefore, not as something foreign to us, but because it is ours — we and all other men having existed as one moral person or one moral whole, in him, and, as the result of that transgression, possessing a nature destitute of love to God and prone to evil."[28] "Adam was once the race; and when he fell, the race fell. Shedd: 'We all existed in Adam in our elementary invisible substance. The *Seyn* of all was there, though the *Daseyn* was not; the *noumenon*, though not the *phenomenon* was in existence.' "[29]

[27] *Ibid.*, pp. 43 f.

[28] Augustus Hopkins Strong: *Systematic Theology* (Philadelphia, 1907), Vol. II, pp. 619 f.

[29] *Ibid.*, p. 621; *cf.* Samuel J. Baird: *The Elohim Revealed in the Creation and Redemption of Man* (Philadelphia, 1860), pp. 305–334; Philip Schaff in John Peter Lange: *A Commentary on the Holy Scriptures* (New York,

It must be acknowledged that if this view were proven to be correct it would adequately explain the two aspects from which the one fact or event may be viewed, namely, that "one sinned" and "all sinned". The question is whether the relevant evidence supports this construction of the Adamic relation.

In dealing with this realistic position and the debate between its proponents and the proponents of the representative view of the relation between Adam and his posterity, it is necessary to place in proper perspective what the crux of the debate is. Sometimes the question is confused by failure to recognize that the proponents of representation as over against realism do not deny but rather maintain that Adam is the natural head as well as the representative head of the race. That is to say, they maintain that the race is seminally one in Adam and that representative union is not to be abstracted from seminal union. Francis Turretine, for example, is quite explicit to this effect. For while holding that the foundation of the imputation of Adam's sin is principally "moral and federal" nevertheless he does not leave out of account the natural headship arising from the unity of origin and the fact that all are of one blood. God willed that Adam should be "the stock and Head of the whole human race" and it is for that reason that "all are said to be one man".[30] What the proponents of the representative headship of Adam insist upon is that the natural or seminal union alone is not sufficient to explain the imputation of Adam's sin to posterity. In this particular respect they are at one with the proponents of realistic union, for the latter also insist on the necessity of more than unity of origin.

Furthermore, not only do the proponents of representation hold to seminal union; they also insist on community of nature. In other words, natural union is involved in natural headship and hence they will say that human nature became

1915), *The Epistle of Paul to the Romans*, pp. 178 f. A. H. Strong's citation of authorities (*op. cit.*, p. 622) is quite unreliable. His appeal to various theologians in support of the realist position is marked by the lack of discrimination which will be shown later on. For example, an examination of H. Martensen: *Christian Dogmatics*, pp. 173–183 or of C. A. Auberlen: *The Divine Revelation*, pp. 175–180 will not disclose the realist position.

[30] *Institutio Theologiae Elencticae, Locus* IX, *Quaestio* IX, §§XI, XII.

corrupt in Adam and that this human nature which became
corrupt in Adam is transmitted to posterity by natural generation. In respect of the term "human nature", then, the difference is not that the proponents of representation deny
community of nature nor do they deny that the human nature
which became corrupt in Adam is propagated to the members
of the race. The difference is simply that realism maintains
the existence in Adam of human nature as an entity that is
specifically and numerically one and at this the exponents of
representation demur.

Hence the crux of the question is not whether the representative view discounts seminal union or natural headship
or community of nature in that unity which exists between
Adam and posterity but simply and solely whether the necessary *plus* which both views posit is to be interpreted in terms
of an entity which existed in its totality in Adam and is
individualized in the members of the race or in terms of a
representation which was established by divine ordination·
It is on that restricted question that the debate must turn.
Other questions undoubtedly emerge in connection with this
restricted question but, relatively, they are subordinate and
peripheral. Confusion can be avoided only if the real crux is
appreciated and debated on the basis of the pertinent data.

When the distinguishing feature of realism is perceived to be
this concept of human nature as *specifically* and *numerically*
one in Adam, the appeal on the part of realists to theologians
of the past in support of this position is not by any means as
valid as it might appear to be. For example, A. H. Strong
says that "Calvin was essentially Augustinian and realistic"
and appeals, in support of this claim, to the *Institutes*, II,
i–iii.[31] Calvin indeed says that all of Adam's posterity became
guilty on account of the fault (culpa) of one. He speaks of the
sin of the one as common.[32] All are dead in Adam, he says,
and are therefore implicated in the ruin of his sin. And, if so,
he likewise maintains, all must be charged with the blame

[31] *Op. cit.*, p. 621; *cf.* also Shedd: *op. cit.*, p. 44.
[32] *Institutio Christianae Religionis*, II, i, 5: "Qua de re multa fuit illis
concertatio, quum a communi sensu nihil magis sit remotum quam ob
unius culpam fieri omnes reos, et ita peccatum fieri commune."

(culpa) of iniquity, for there is no condemnation when there is no blame (culpa).[33] Adam plunged all his progeny into the same miseries to which he himself became heir. (If we give to such expressions the fullest scope and interpret them as implying that the one sin of Adam is the sin of all, there is no proof that Calvin conceived of the union existing between Adam and posterity in realistic terms. Calvin, however, does not leave us in doubt as to his understanding of the involvement of posterity in the sin of Adam, or, in other words, how the sin of Adam becomes the sin of all. Calvin was not unaware of the objection urged against the doctrine that the sin of Adam involved the race in ruin, namely, that posterity is charged with the guilt of a sin which is the sin of another and not their own personal transgression.[34] But he did not meet this objection by saying that the sin in question was not only the sin of Adam but also of that human nature, specifically and numerically one, which existed in its undivided totality in Adam and belonged to each member of the race as well as to Adam himself. He did not appeal to the participation of such an entity in the first sin of Adam. And there need not be doubt as to his positive answer to the question how we become involved in the sin of Adam; he does not weary of reiteration. It is to the effect that we derive from Adam by natural generation and propagation a corrupt nature. The key concept is that of hereditary depravity. Adam by his sin corrupted his nature and we all from our birth are infected with that contagion.[35] "We hear that the uncleanness of the parents is transmitted to the children so that all without any exception are defiled from their beginning. But we shall not find the origin of this pollution unless we ascend to the first parent of all, as to the fountain. Thus it is certain that Adam was not only the progenitor of human nature but as it were the root,

[33] *Inst.* II, i, 6: "Qui nos omnes in Adam mortuos esse pronuntiat, jam simul aperte quoque testatur, peccati labe esse implicitos. Neque enim ad eos perveniret damnatio qui nulla iniquitatis culpa attingerentur."

[34] *Idem*: "Neque id suo unius vitio, quod nihil ad nos pertineat; sed quoniam universum suum semen ea, in quam lapsus erat, vitiositate infecit."

[35] *Ibid.*, II, i, 5: "Omnes ergo qui ab impuro semine descendimus peccati contagione nascimur infecti."

and therefore the human race was vitiated in his corruption."[36]
Adam "infected all his seed with that vitiosity into which he
had fallen".[37] "Hence from a rotten root spring rotten branches
which transmit their rottenness to other twigs which spring
from them."[38] The figure is obviously that of contagion
spreading from a corrupted source. And Calvin is even careful
to say that Adam's own personal corruption does not pertain
to us; it is simply that he infects us with the depravity into
which he had lapsed.[39] Indubitably, therefore, according to
Calvin, the sin by which posterity is ruined is the depravity
which *stems* from the sin of Adam, the corrupted human
nature which is the *consequence* of Adam's apostasy and which
is communicated to and transfused into us by propagation.
And it is not without some significance that he appeals to
Augustine in support of his contention. "Therefore good men,
and above all others Augustine, have laboured on this point
to show that we are corrupted not by acquired wickedness but
that we bring innate depravity from our mother's womb."[40]

It is not our purpose now to maintain that Calvin has given
an adequate account of the relation of the race to the one sin
of Adam. Our interest now is merely to show that his emphasis
upon hereditary depravity, and the corruption of our nature
which emanates from the sin of Adam, is no proof that Calvin
held the realist conception of the Adamic union. The representative view of our relation to Adam maintains insist-
ently all that Calvin propounds respecting the propagation of
hereditary depravity and does so in Calvinian terms.

Realists also appeal with confidence to Augustine as a
proponent of the realist position. It is not our interest or
intent to demonstrate that Augustine did not entertain realist
conceptions. It is necessary, however, to point out that the
statements of Augustine on this subject, quoted or cited by
the proponents of realism, are not conclusive in this connec-

---

[36] *Ibid.*, II, i, 6.

[37] *Idem.*

[38] *Ibid.*, II, i, 7: "Proinde a radice putrefacta rami putridi prodierunt,
qui suam putredinem transmiserunt ad alios ex se nascentes surculos."

[39] *Ibid.*, II, i, 6.

[40] *Ibid.*, II, i, 5: "Nos non ascita nequitia corrumpi, sed ingenitam
vitiositatem ab utero matris afferre."

tion. Augustine does say that "all sinned, since all were that one man".[41] And perhaps the following offers more apparent support than any other to a realist interpretation of Augustine's position. "For God, the author of natures, not of vices, created man upright; but man, being of his own will corrupted, and justly condemned, begat corrupted and condemned children. For we all were in that one man, since we all were that one man, who fell into sin by the woman who was made from him before the sin. For not yet was the particular form created and distributed to us, in which we as individuals were to live, but already the seminal nature was there from which we were to be propagated; and this being vitiated by sin, and bound by the chain of death, and justly condemned, man could not be born of man in another condition. And thus, from the bad use of free will, there arose the train of this calamity which leads the human race by a combination of miseries from its depraved origin, as from a corrupt root, to the destruction of the second death, which has no end, those only being excepted who are freed by the grace of God."[42] When, however, the contexts of such quotations as these are examined it will be observed that the paramount interest of Augustine, as of Calvin, is to deny that it is by *imitation* that the one offence of Adam is unto the condemnation of all and to prove that it is by *propagation* that sin was transmitted from the first man to other men.[43] Referring to Paul he writes: " 'By one man', he says, 'sin entered into the world, and death by sin.' This speaks of propagation, not of imitation: for if it were by imitation, he would have said, 'by the devil'."[44] "As therefore, He, in whom all are made alive, besides offering himself as an example of righteousness to those who imitate Him, gives also to those who believe on Him the hidden grace of His Spirit, which He secretly infuses even into infants; so likewise he, in whom all die, besides being an example for

---

[41] *De Peccatorum Meritis et Remissione,* I, x, 11: "in quo omnes peccaverunt; quando omnes ille unus homo fuerunt"; *cf. ibid.,* III, vii, 14.

[42] *De Civitate Dei,* XIII, xiv; *cf. ibid.,* XIII, iii. With slight variation the translation is that of Marcus Dods in *A Select Library of the Nicene and Post-Nicene Fathers* (Buffalo, 1887).

[43] *Cf. De Pec. Mer. et Rem.,* I, ix, 9.

[44] *Ibid.,* I, ix, 10.

imitation to those who wilfully transgress the commandment of the Lord, depraved also in his own person all who come of his stock by the hidden corruption of his own carnal concupiscence. It is entirely on this account, and for no other reason, that the apostle says: 'By one man sin entered into the world, and death by sin, and so passed upon all men; in which all have sinned.' "[45]

Consequently, although Augustine says that all of Adam's posterity were that one man, that the whole human race was in the first man,[46] and that all sinned in Adam when as yet they were that one man,[47] nevertheless when he defines more specifically the sin by which all sinned in Adam and through which death passed to all he does so in terms of original sin or hereditary depravity passed on from Adam to his seed by propagation. The reason why posterity is said to have sinned in Adam is that the "seminal nature",[48] from which all were to be propagated, had been defiled in Adam when as yet it existed only in him. And so, when Augustine exegetes Romans 5:12 and particularly "in whom all sinned", his most defining concept is that Adam "depraved . . . in himself by the hidden corruption of his carnal concupiscence all who come of his stock"[49] and that this defilement is propagated by natural generation.

When this is recognized it is not so apparent that Augustine's thought follows the realist pattern. In the last analysis he falls back on the notion of original sin as prop-

---

[45] *Idem*, as translated in *A Select Library of the Nicene and Post-Nicene Fathers* (New York, 1887).

[46] *De Civ. Dei*, XIII, iii: "In primo igitur homine per feminam in progeniem transiturum universum genus humanum fuit, quando illa conjugum copula divinam sententiam suae damnationis excepit."

[47] *De Pec. Mer. et Rem.*, III, vii, 14: "Unde nec illud liquide dici potest, quod peccatum Adae etiam non peccantibus nocuit, cum Scriptura dicat, *in quo omnes peccaverunt*. Nec sic dicuntur ista aliena peccata, tanquam omnino ad parvulos non pertineant: siquidem in Adam omnes tunc peccaverunt, quando in ejus natura illa insita vi qua eos gignere poterat, adhuc omnes ille unus fuerunt: sed dicuntur aliena, quia nondum ipsi agebant vitas proprias, sed quidquid erat in futura propagine, vita unius hominis continebat."

[48] *Cf. De Civ. Dei*, XIII, xiv.

[49] *De Pec. Mer. et Rem.*, I, ix, 10.

agated. And we must bear in mind that the concept of human
nature as defiled in Adam and transmitted to posterity by
propagation is not the monopoly of the realist. The proponent
of representation holds as tenaciously to that doctrine as does
the realist. While it is granted that some of Augustine's
expressions could readily fall into the realist construction of
the Adamic union, there is no clear-cut or conclusive evidence
in these quotations that he conceived of the rationale of our
involvement in Adam's sin as consisting in the *participation*
of human nature, as specifically and numerically one, in the
sin of Adam. He conceived indeed of human nature as having
become depraved in Adam and as communicated to us. But
these two are not identical and to fail to distinguish them
leads only to confusion and to misapprehension of the *status
quaestionis*.

If the distinguishing feature of realism has been brought
into focus and if the question at issue has been placed in
proper perspective, we may now address ourselves to the
examination of realism as it applies to our topic. It may be
repeated that if realism were shown to be correct it would
provide an adequate explanation of the two ways in which
the one event may be viewed, namely, that *"one* sinned" and
yet *"all* sinned". However, is there evidence to support this
construction of the relationship of the one to the many?

(i) W. G. T. Shedd maintains that it is unreasonable to
regard representative union of Adam and posterity as a proper
basis for the imputation of Adam's sin, because such imputation would be "an arbitrary act of sovereignty". But, we are
compelled to ask, does the notion of human nature, specifically and numerically one, human nature as an "elementary
invisible substance", in any way relieve the difficulty entailed?
For the real question is how the individual members of the
race can bear the guilt of a sin in which they did not, *as
individuals*, personally and voluntarily participate. And the
realist has to admit that the individual members of the race
did not *personally* and *individually* participate in the sin of
this human nature as it existed in its unity in Adam. The
sin of generic humanity is just as far removed from the
individual sin of the members of posterity as is the sin of a
representative head and that for the simple reason that *as*

individuals posterity did not yet exist. In other words, it is as difficult to establish the nexus between the sin of generic humanity and the members of the race as it is to establish the nexus between the sin of Adam as representative head and the members of the race. After all, generic humanity as it existed in Adam is impersonal unindividualized human nature.

(ii) The analogy instituted in Romans 5:12–19 (*cf.* I Cor. 15:22) presents a formidable objection to the realist construction. It is admitted by the realist that there is no "realistic" union between Christ and the justified. That is to say, there is no human nature, specifically and numerically one, existing in its unity in Christ, which is individualized in those who are the beneficiaries of Christ's righteousness. On realist premises, therefore, a radical disparity must be posited between the character of the union that exists between Adam and his posterity, on the one hand, and the union that exists between Christ and those who are his, on the other. In Romans 5:15–19 the differences between the reign of sin, condemnation, and death and the reign of righteousness, justification, and life are in the forefront; they are evident from the negations of verses 15–17 and from the emphasis placed upon the superabundance that prevails in the provisions of grace. But there is no hint of the kind of discrepancy that would obtain if the distinction between the nature of the union in the two cases were as radical as realism must suppose. This argument from silence might carry little weight of itself. But the case is not merely that there is no hint of this kind of difference; the sustained parallelism militates against any such supposition. Adam is the type of the one to come (vs. 14). Adam as the one is parallel to Jesus Christ as the one (vs. 17). The one trespass unto condemnation is parallel to the one righteousness unto justification (vs. 18). The disobedience of the one is parallel to the obedience of the one (vs. 19). This sustained emphasis not only upon the one man Adam and the one man Christ but also upon the one trespass and the one righteous act points to a basic identity in respect of *modus operandi*. But if, in the one case, we have a oneness that is focused in the unity of the human nature, which realism posits, and, in the other case, a oneness that is focused in the one man Jesus Christ, where no *such* unity exists, it is difficult not to believe that discrepancy enters at the very point where similitude must be maintained. For, after all, on realist assumptions, it is not our union with Adam that is the crucial consideration in our involvement in his sin but our involvement in the sin of that human nature which existed in Adam. And what the parallelism of Romans 5:12-19 would indicate is that the one sin of the one man Adam is analogous on the side of condemnation to the one righteousness of the one man Jesus Christ on the side of justification. The kind of relationship that obtains in the one case obtains in the other. And how can this be if the kind of relationship is so different in respect of the *nature* of the union subsisting?

It is not a valid objection to the foregoing argument drawn from the parallelism in Romans 5:12-19 to say that, since there is an incontestable distinction between the relation of Adam to the race and the relation of Christ to his own, there is no reason why the further distinction which realism posits should be inconsistent with the parallelism of the passage concerned. The distinction which cannot be questioned is that Adam sustains a genetic relation to the whole race and that all are seminally united with and derived from him. This does not hold in the relation of Christ to his people. But the reason why this consideration does not affect the argument is that, in terms of the debate between the realist and the representationist, it is not the fact of seminal, genetic relationship that constitutes the specific ground of our involvement in the one sin of the one man Adam either for the realist or for the exponent of representation. For the realist it is realistic union; for the representationist it is representative union. And in the matter of Romans 5:12-19 it is the question of the ground upon which the one sin of Adam is unto the condemnation of all and the one righteousness of Christ unto the justification of all who are Christ's. Neither the realist nor the representationist holds that the ground in the case of Adam's sin is the fact that Adam is the natural progenitor of the race. Both are concerned with the *specific ground* of the imputation of Adam's sin, and, in respect of the parallel drawn in Romans 5:12-19, the question is whether the *specific ground* posited by the realist for this imputation is compatible with the analogy which is instituted by the apostle between the one sin of the one man unto condemnation and the one righteousness of the one man Jesus Christ unto justification. The specific character of the union which is the specific ground of condemnation and justification is the question at issue.

(iii) When we ask the question as to the evidence provided by Scripture for the existence in Adam of this "elementary invisible substance" called human nature construed as specifically and numerically one, we are at a loss to find it. We are truly one in Adam, in terms of Hebrews 7:9, 10 we were all in the loins of Adam, he is the first parent of all mankind, and seminally there is the unity of Adam and his posterity. Adam was the first endowed with human nature and to all his offspring he has transmitted that human nature by natural procreation. All of this is maintained by representationists as well as by realists and finds support in Scripture. But the additional postulate on the part of the realist, the postulate indispensable to his distinctive position, is not one that can plead the support of biblical evidence. And it is not a postulate that is necessary to explain the facts brought to our attention in the biblical revelation. The union that exists between Adam and posterity is one that can be interpreted in terms for which there is sufficient evidence in the data of revelation available to us.

(iv) The argument of the realist to the effect that only the doctrine of the specific unity of the race in Adam lays a proper basis in justice for the imputation to posterity of the sin of Adam and his contention that the imputation to posterity of the sin of a vicarious representative violates the order of justice[50] do not take sufficient account of what is involved in our solidaric or corporate relationships. Realists admit that only in the case of Adam and posterity does their postulate of specific unity hold true. And solidaric relationship, they must likewise admit, exists in other institutions where the specific unity exemplified in Adam is not present at all. But, if we analyse the responsibilities entailed in these other solidaric relationships and assess the same in scriptural terms, we shall find that moral responsibility devolves upon the members of a corporate entity by virtue of the actions of the representatives

[50] Cf. Shedd: op. cit., p. 36.

or the representative of that entity.[51] Consequently the denial of the imputation of vicarious sin runs counter to the way in which the principle of solidarity operates in other spheres. And it is not valid to insist that vicarious sin can be imputed only when there is the *voluntary* engagement to undertake such imputation.[52] Corporate relationship exists by divine institution and the corporate responsibilities exist and come to effect apart altogether from voluntary engagement on the part of the persons concerned to assume these responsibilities. It is only because we fail to take account of the pervasiveness of corporate responsibility and think too lightly of the implications of this responsibility that we might be ready to accede to the argument that there cannot be the imputation to us of the sin of a vicarious representative. As the principle applies to Adam it is not difficult to see that imputation of sin on the basis of Adam's representative capacity could operate with unique and universal application. For this would be but the extension to the whole race, in terms of its solidarity in Adam, of a principle which is exemplified constantly in more restricted corporate relationships.

2. *The Representative View*

In presenting and defending the representative view it is necessary to relieve it of some misrepresentation on the part of opponents and of certain extravagances on the part of proponents. With reference to the latter, as will be shown later in this series of studies, the representative view is not bound up with the assumption that posterity is involved only in the *poena* of Adam's sin and not in the *culpa*. It is not to be supposed that only realism can hold to the imputation of the

---

[51] It is purely gratuitous to say, as Shedd does, that "representative union requires and supposes the consent of the individuals who are to be represented" (*ibid.*, p. 39). This is not the case in some of the solidaric relationships which exist among men by divine constitution. In the state, for example, it is a fallacy to suppose that the solidarity arises simply and solely from the consent of the citizens or subjects. The state is a divine ordinance and its sanctions and responsibilities do not emanate from voluntary contract on the part of the members.

[52] *Cf.* Shedd: *ibid.*, p. 57.

culpa of Adam's transgression. Furthermore, the representative view is not to be loaded with the distinction between *reatus culpae* and *reatus poenae* which the older Reformed theologians rejected and which they characterized and criticized as papistical. With reference to misrepresentation or at least misconception on the part of opponents, it may not be unnecessary to repeat that the representative view does not deny but rather affirms the natural headship of Adam, the seminal union of Adam and posterity, that all derive from Adam by natural generation a corrupt nature, and that therefore original sin is passed on by propagation. W. G. T. Shedd says: "Since the idea of representation by Adam is incompatible with that of specific existence in Adam, the choice must be made between representative union and natural union. A combination of the two views is illogical."[53] It is true that in terms of Shedd's definition of natural union as that of specific existence in Adam there cannot be a combination of the two ideas in the explanation of the imputation of Adam's sin to posterity; to say the least, one idea makes superfluous the other. And it is also true that the representative idea finds in representation rather than in natural headship the *specific* ground of the imputation of Adam's sin. In this respect there is similarity to the realist distinction, because realists find in the specific unity rather than in Adam's parenthood the *specific* ground of the imputation of Adam's sin. But it is quite illogical to maintain that on the representationist view of Adam's natural headship there is any incompatibility between natural headship and representative union. On the representative construction natural headship and represent-

---

[53] *Ibid.*, p. 39; *cf.* pp. 37 f. It should be noted, however, that realists do not refrain from speaking of Adam as the representative head of the human race. Philip Schaff says: "Adam fell, not as an individual simply, but as the real representative head of the human race" (*op. cit.*, p. 179). And A. H. Strong: "Only on this supposition of Natural Headship could God justly constitute Adam our representative, or hold us responsible for the depraved nature we have received from him" (*op. cit.*, p. 623). This use of the word "representative", however, is in their esteem based upon the conception of the specific unity of the race in Adam and does not have associated with it the distinguishing connotation attached to it by those maintaining the representative view in distinction from and opposition to the realist.

ative headship are correlative, and each aspect has its own proper and specific function in the explanation of the status and condition in which the members of the race find themselves in consequence of their relation to Adam. Hence it must be appreciated that emphasis upon the natural headship of Adam and upon the seminal union of Adam and his posterity in Reformed theologians is not to be interpreted as vacillation between two incompatible ideas,[54] nor is appeal to natural headship and seminal relationship on the part of such theologians to be regarded as the espousal of the realist construction.[55]

When we come to the question of the evidence in support of the representative view it is necessary to adduce in more positive fashion considerations mentioned already in the criticism of realism.

(i) The natural or seminal union between Adam and posterity is not in question; it is assumed. It might be argued that this is all that is necessary and that Scripture does not clearly establish any additional kind of union, that as Levi paid tithes when he was in the loins of Abraham, so posterity sinned in the loins of Adam.[56] Why postulate more? Some *plus*, however, appears to be demanded. It may not be questioned that there is something severely unique and distinct about our involvement in the sin of Adam. The sin is the *one* sin of Adam. If the relationship to Adam were simply that of seminal union, that of being in his loins, this would not provide any explanation why the sin imputed is the first sin *alone*.

---

[54] *Cf*. Shedd: *op. cit.*, p. 36.

[55] *Cf*. Shedd's interpretation of Calvin in this regard (*ibid.*, p. 44).

[56] The Westminster Confession of Faith may appear to ground the imputation of Adam's sin upon the seminal relationship in Chapter VI, iii, when, referring to our first parents, it says: "They being the root of all mankind, the guilt of this sin was imputed; and the same death in sin, and corrupted nature, conveyed to all their posterity descending from them by ordinary generation". The Larger Catechism, however, grounds the imputation of Adam's sin upon the covenant institution. "The covenant being made with Adam as a publick person, not for himself only, but for his posterity, all mankind descending from him by ordinary generation, sinned in him, and fell with him in that first transgression" (Q. 22; *cf*. The Shorter Catechism, Q. 16). How the difference is to be explained is another question into which it is not necessary to enter now.

We were as much in his loins when he committed other sins
and these other sins would be just as applicable to us as his
first sin if the whole explanation of the imputation of his first
sin resides in the fact that we were in his loins. Hence some
additional factor is required to explain the restriction to the
one sin of Adam. In the light of the narrative in Genesis 2
and 3 we shall have to infer that the prohibition of the tree
of the knowledge of good and evil was associated with and
epitomised some special relationship that was constituted by
divine institution and by reason of which the trespass or
disobedience of Adam in this particular involved not only
Adam but all of his posterity by natural generation. In other
words, there was a special act of providence by which a special
relationship was constituted in terms of which we are to
interpret the implications for posterity of that one trespass of
Adam in partaking of the forbidden fruit.

(ii) In I Corinthians 15:22, 45–49 Paul provides us with
what is one of the most striking and significant rubrics in all
of Scripture. He comprehends God's dealings with men under
the twofold headship of the two Adams. There is none before
Adam; he is the first man. There is none between Adam and
Christ, for Christ is the second man. There is none after
Christ; he is the last Adam (vss. 45–47). Adam and Christ
sustain unique relations to men. And that history and destiny
are determined by these relationships is demonstrated by
verse 22: "As in Adam all die, even so in Christ all shall be
made alive". All who die die in Adam; all who are made alive
are made alive in Christ. In view of this comprehensive
philosophy of human history and destiny and in view of the
pivotal and determinative roles of the first and last Adam,
we must posit constitutive ordination on God's part to these
unique relationships. And since the analogy instituted between Adam and Christ is so conspicuous, it is surely necessary
to assume that the kind of relationship which Adam sustains
to men is after the pattern of the relationship which Christ
sustains to men. To put the case conversely, surely the kind
of relationship that Christ sustains to men is after the pattern
which Adam sustains to men (cf. Rom. 5:14). But if all that
we posit in the case of Adam is simply his natural headship or
parenthood, we do not have the kind of relationship that

would provide the pattern for the headship of Christ. Hence the analogy would require some community of relationship which the natural headship of Adam does not provide.

(iii) As noted already, Romans 5:12–19 furnishes more evidence relevant to the question at issue than any other passage. The fact that Adam is the type of the one to come (vs. 14) and the sustained parallelism throughout the succeeding verses (vss. 15–19) imply some similarity of relationship. And when we ask the question what this common principle is there are three things to be said. (a) In the relation of Adam to posterity we must posit more than natural headship, for the simple reason that, as we found above, this kind of union provides no analogy to the union that exists between Christ and his people. (b) In the case of Christ and the justified we know that the union is that of vicarious representation. In the provisions of grace Christ has been ordained to act for and in the place of those who are the beneficiaries of redemption. His righteousness becomes theirs unto their justification and eternal life. This is a constitution that exists by divine institution, and the whole process which negates the reign of sin, condemnation, and death rests upon the union thereby constituted. (c) The general thrust as well as the details of the passage would indicate that a similar kind of relationship exists in the reign of sin, condemnation, and death. The passage is built upon the contrast between the reign of sin, condemnation, and death, on the one hand, as proceeding from the sin of Adam, and the reign of righteousness, justification, and life, on the other, as proceeding from the righteousness of Christ. We are compelled to recognize an identity of *modus operandi* because Adam is the type of Christ. Why, we may ask, should we seek for any other principle in terms of which the reign of sin, condemnation, and death operates than the principle which is exemplified in the reign of righteousness, justification, and life? We cannot posit less. Why should we posit more when there is no evidence to demand or support it?

We conclude, therefore, that more than natural headship is necessary, that natural headship does not carry with it the notion of "specific unity" in Adam, that the *plus* required to explain the imputation of Adam's *first* sin and no other is not shown by Scripture to be the kind of union which realism postulates, and that when we seek to discover the specific character of the union which will ground the imputation of Adam's first sin we find it to be that same kind of union as is analogous to the union that exists between Christ and his people and on the basis of which his righteousness is theirs unto justification and eternal life. How we should denominate this kind of union is a matter of terminology. If we call it representative union or headship, this will suffice for identification purposes. Solidarity was constituted by divine institution and the solidarity is of such a nature that the sin of Adam devolves upon all naturally procreated posterity.

CHAPTER THREE

IV. THE NATURE OF THE IMPUTATION

IF THE union existing between Adam and his posterity is analogous to that which exists between Christ and his people and may thus be called representative union, the next question that arises is that of the mode by which the sin of Adam comes to be reckoned to the account of posterity. Discussion of this question is required by exegetical and theological considerations, particularly by the data implicit in Romans 5:12–19. But the history of debate on this question compels us to deal with it, even if we were disposed to discount or ignore the exegetical data. And history in this case, as in so many others, dictates the direction in which the discussion must be turned. There are two viewpoints which, in contrast with each other, serve to bring the question into the perspective that throws a flood of light upon the significance of the exegetical data.

1. *Mediate Imputation*

The name particularly associated with the doctrine of mediate imputation is that of Josua Placaeus (Josué de la Place) of the Reformed school at Saumur. He was understood to have taught that original sin consisted simply in the depravity derived from Adam and did not include the imputation of the guilt of Adam's first sin. The Twenty-Eighth Synod of the Reformed Churches in France, meeting at Charenton from December 26, 1644 to January 26, 1645, officially condemned this doctrine in the following terms. "There was a report made in the Synod of a certain writing, both printed and manuscript, holding forth this doctrine, that the whole nature of original sin consisted only in that corruption, which is hereditary to all Adam's posterity, and residing originally in all men, and denieth the imputation of his first sin. The Synod condemneth the said doctrine as far as it restraineth the nature of original sin to the sole hereditary corruption of Adam's posterity, to the excluding of the imputation of that first sin by which he fell, and interdicteth on pain of all Church-censures all pastors, professors, and others, who shall treat of this question, to depart from the common received opinion of the Protestant Churches, who (over and besides that corruption) have all acknowledged the imputation of Adam's first sin unto his posterity."[57] Placaeus replied to this decree of the Synod by maintaining that he did not deny the imputation to posterity of Adam's first sin and that therefore he was in entire accord with the Synod's decree in not restricting original sin to hereditary corruption. What he maintained was that the imputation of Adam's first sin was *mediate*, not *immediate*. Immediate and antecedent imputation, he contended, must be distinguished from mediate and consequent. The former takes place immediately and is not mediated by hereditary corruption; the latter takes place mediately and is mediated by this corruption. In the former case the imputation of Adam's first sin precedes corruption in the order of nature and is reckoned to be the cause of corruption; in the latter case the imputation of the first sin follows hereditary corruption and is reckoned to be the effect. Immediate imputation Placaeus rejected and mediate imputation he espoused. In a word his position was that the imputation to posterity of Adam's first sin was mediated through the inheritance from him of a corrupt nature.[58]

[57] *Synodicon in Gallia Reformata: or, the Acts, Decisions, Decrees, and Canons of those Famous National Councils of the Reformed Churches in France*, ed. John Quick (London, 1692), vol. II, p. 473.

[58] Placaeus deals with the question in an extensive treatise, *De Imputatione Primi Peccati Adami Disputatio Bipertita* in which he deals with the decree of the Synod of Charenton and with the theologians who had controverted his position as well as with others of the past and contemporary with himself who, he claimed, supported his contentions. This treatise in two parts is found in his *Opera Omnia* (Franeker, 1699), Tom. I, pp. 159–479. The following quotations will serve as examples of his distinction between immediate and mediate imputation. "Sin vero per primum Adae peccatum, primum ejus peccatum actuale intelligitur . . .

It is not surprising that Placaeus should have been understood to deny altogether the imputation of Adam's first sin. For in several places in his works, even subsequent to the decree of the Synod of Charenton, he explicitly contends against the doctrine of the imputation to posterity of the actual first sin of Adam whether this imputation is conceived of as *culpa* or *poena*.[59] And it is understandable that the

distinguenda est imputatio in imputationem immediatam seu antecedentem, et imputationem mediatam seu consequentem: illa fit immediate, hoc est, non mediante corruptione; haec fit mediate, hoc est, mediante corruptione haereditaria. Illa ordine naturae corruptionem antecedit; haec sequitur. Illa corruptionis causa censetur esse, haec effectum. Illam Placeus rejicit, hanc admittit" (*Opera Omnia*, I, p. 173).

"Potest enim animo concipi duplex imputatio. *Immediata* et *Mediata* . . . . Immediatam voco eam, quam solam Thesibus, quas tu refutandas tibi sumpsisti, negare volui; qua putatur *actio* illa Adami, hoc est, vetiti fructus manducatio ejus posteris omnibus (Christo excepto) proxime, immediate, hoc ipso quod filii sunt Adami, imputari ad duas istas poenas proprie dictas, privationem justitiae originalis quam mortem spiritualem appellas, et mortem aeternam. Hanc solam imputationem actionis illius ego negavi, quia non docetur in Sacris literis adequata fidei nostrae norma, quia pugnat cum Sacris literis, quia Deum facit authorem peccati, quia Dei justitiam dehonestat, quia sequitur ex ea Christum esse natura sua peccatorem, quia alia nonnulla trahit secum absurda, mirabilem religionis Christianae puritatem et splendorem obscurantia, quae utinam fratres et conservi nostri a me per theses moniti, aut non prorsus contempsissent, aut non contemptim expendissent!

"Mediatam seu consequentem appello eam, quae haereditariae corruptionis in nos ab Adamo derivatae intuitum consequitur, eaque mediante fit. Hujus enim corruptionis participatione communicamus peccato Adami, eique, ut ita loquar, habitualiter consentimus, ac propterea digni sumus, qui Adamo peccatori annumeremur" (*ibid.*, p. 280).

"Quaeritur, *Utrum primum peccatum actuale Adami praecise sumptum, nobis ejus posteris imputetur a Deo justo judice proxime, immediate ac ordine naturae priusquam inhaerenter corrupti simus?* Tu venerande Frater affirmas: ego nego" (*ibid.*, p. 281).

[59] "Quandocunque igitur Deus nobis peccatum originis *imputare* dicatur, sive cum sumus, sive antequam simis, sive in tempore, sive ab aeterno, id peccatum aliud nihil est quam inhaerens illud a nativitate nobis vitium, quod a primo nostro parente non per *imputationem*, sed per carnalem generationem traximus" (*ibid.*, p. 442). "Denique de jure non magis ad me *poena* Adami pertinet quam *culpa* (*ibid.*, p. 291). "Cum enim affirmo, peccatum actuale Adami nobis non imputari, non hoc volo, peccatum illud non considerari ut peccatum, sed tegi, condonari, et remitti nobis . . . . Sed, quicquid fit, contendo peccatum illud Adami actuale nostrum peccatum

critics of Placaeus' position should aver that mediate imputation as propounded by him is tantamount to a denial of the
imputation to posterity of Adam's *first* sin.[60]

In the debate that ensued upon the issuance of the decree
of the Synod Placaeus was to a very large extent concerned
with his opponent Garissolius but also with others, the most
notable of whom were Andrew Rivetus and Samuel Maresius.
Rivetus wrote a rather lengthy treatise[61] which largely consists
of quotations from the creeds of the protestant churches and
from protestant theologians. A large number of these quotations do not bear precisely upon the point of the distinction
later propounded by Placaeus in his *Disputatio*. Some of
them do not even bear upon the question of the imputation
of Adam's first sin but are concerned with the doctrine of
original sin or inherent depravity. But a considerable number
of the quotations are directly germane to the question raised
by Placaeus' distinction, in that they expressly assert the
priority of the imputation of Adam's first sin. Apparently
Rivetus' purpose was not to maintain that *all* these quotations

non esse. Itaque nobis jure imputari non posse" (*ibid.*, p. 307). "Tribus
autem modis communicari potest peccatum, docendo, imputando, et pro-
pagando generatione naturali. Non communicavit (Adamus) autem docendo . . . . Non communicavit etiam imputatione; nam nec imputatio est
actio Adami, nec actio justi judicis peccatorem facit . . . . Communicavit
igitur propagatione naturali, transmisso per generationem carnalem semine,
quam naturae, tam vitiositatis naturae . . . . Haec corruptio peccatum est,
non quidem actuale, sed habituale, et voluntaria est, non ut actio, sed ut
qualitas, hoc est, non quia est a voluntate, sed quia est in voluntate"
(*ibid.*, pp. 708 f.).

   60 *Cf*. Francis Turretine who says of mediate imputation: "Verum si
penitus res attendatur, non obscure patebit distinctionem istam ad fucum
faciendum esse excogitatam, quae nomen imputationis retinendo, rem
ipsam de facto tollit. Nam si ideo tantum Adae peccatum nobis imputari
dicitur mediate, quia apud Deum rei constituimur, et obnoxii poenae fimus
propter corruptionem haereditariam quam ab Adamo trahimus, nulla erit
imputatio proprie peccati Adami, sed tantum labis inhaerentis" (*Institutio
Theologiae Elencticae*, Loc. IX, Quaest. IX, § VI).

   61 *Decretum Synodi Nationalis Ecclesiarum Reformatarum Galliae initio
Anni 1645 de Imputatione Primi Peccati Omnibus Adami Posteris* (see
Opera Theologica, Rotterdam, 1660, Tom. III, pp. 798–823). See the
English translation of some of Rivetus' quotations by Charles Hodge in
Theological Essays: Reprinted from the Princeton Review (New York, 1846),
pp. 196–217.

referred to the distinction which the Synod made between the imputation of Adam's first sin and the hereditary depravity derived from him, far less that they all upheld the antecedence of the guilt of Adam's first sin. We can only infer that he set forth a great variety of quotations, many of which supported the distinction which the Synod had formulated and with which Placaeus later professed himself to be in full agreement, and some of which were clearly in conflict with the position later enunciated by Placaeus, namely, that of the consequent or posterior imputation of Adam's first sin.[62] Whatever may be said of the validity of Placaeus' contention in the last two chapters of his *Disputatio* to the effect that the Confessions of the Reformed Churches do not favour the doctrine of the immediate imputation of Adam's first sin and that, further-more, this doctrine is alien to that of the early reformers, it was not difficult for him to show that such creeds as the Gallic, Belgic, Scottish, and Helvetic did not formulate a doctrine of immediate imputation and could not therefore be appealed to in support of the same.[63]

The viewpoint propounded by Placaeus and the debate provoked by it exercised a profound influence upon subsequent thought on the whole question. Theologians like Heidegger and Turretine in the seventeenth century used their polemic talents in opposition to the doctrine of mediate imputation. In the matter of creedal formulation the most significant fact is that the *Formula Consensus Helvetica* (1675) declared ex-plicitly in favour of the doctrine of immediate imputation.[64]

---

[62] The priority of the imputation of Adam's first sin appears quite plainly, for example, in the quotations from William Bucanus, Amandus Polanus, Theodore Beza, Lambertus Danaeus Aurelius, and Robert Rollock. The main thesis of Rivetus' treatise, namely, that the distinction set forth by the Synod of Charenton was the common sentiment of the Protestant Churches, the quotations bear out. With this thesis, of course, Placaeus did not profess to be in disagreement. It has to be borne in mind, however, that it was in support of the Synod's distinction that Rivetus compiled his testimonies, whereas Placaeus' *Disputatio* is devoted to a refutation of *immediate* imputation. But since some of the quotations bear directly upon this latter question Rivetus' treatise is of considerable value in reference to the debate on immediate imputation.

[63] *Cf.* Placaeus: *op. cit.*, pp. 446–459.

[64] *Formula Consensus Helvetica*, Canones X, XI, XII.

Mediate imputation also enlisted its advocates in the centuries that followed. On the continent of Europe the names of Campegius Vitringa, Hermann Venema, and J. F. Stapfer are usually listed as exponents of mediate imputation.[65] In the United States of America mediate imputation was adopted by certain New England theologians of the eighteenth century and was one of the tenets of the new school theology in the Presbyterian Church in the nineteenth century. As representative of the latter, Henry B. Smith vigorously opposed immediate imputation[66] and sets forth mediate imputation as the position which, in his esteem, does more justice to the facts of the case.[67] In dealing with the developments which took place among the New England theologians it is necessary to enter into more detail. For though there is an affinity with the doctrine of mediate imputation as formulated by Placaeus, yet so many marked differences had appeared that the doctrine of mediate imputation, as historically understood, can scarcely be regarded as a proper description of the viewpoint entertained. The case might be more accurately described as one of decided opposition to the doctrine of immediate imputation, an opposition which served as a starting-point for a construction which is in some respects similar to that of

[65] With reference to Campegius Vitringa the elder the only reflection on the question that I have been able to find in his published works is that in his *Doctrina Christianae Religionis per Apharismos Summatim Descripta* (Leyden, 1762), edited by Martinus Vitringa, in which he says: "Qui reatus, an a primo Adàmi peccato *mediate*, an *immediate* pendeat, in scholis subtilius magis, quam utilius disputatur; cum eadem utrobique res teneatur, et adversus Pelagianizantes asseratur. Id certum, intervenisse hic Dei judicium, et posse proinde hoc consequens peccati protoplastorum, in eorum posteris, hoc sensu appelari peccatum originale imputatum" (Pars II, pp. 347 f.) This would indicate that Vitringa was not very jealous for one position against another in the dispute. The long and informative note by Martinus Vitringa in the same volume (pp. 349–354) provides a survey of the debate in the seventeenth century and of the theologians involved. The English translation of Venema's *Institutes of Theology* by Alex. W. Brown (Andover, 1853) clearly shows that Venema espoused mediate imputation (*cf.* pp. 518 ff.). With Stapfer's position we shall deal later in connection with Jonathan Edwards.

[66] Henry B. Smith: *System of Christian Theology* (New York, 1888), pp. 304–308.

[67] *Ibid.*, pp. 314 ff.

mediate imputation but which in the course of development meant the complete abandonment of the notion of the imputation to posterity of Adam's first sin.

Samuel Hopkins is explicit to the effect "that the sin, and the consequent guilt and condemnation of all the human race, were by divine constitution connected with Adam's sinning",[68] that "by virtue of the covenant and constitution made with the father of mankind" all men "fell under condemnation to death" and "are become wholly corrupt and sinful".[69] Hence "the sin and ruin of all mankind was implied and certainly involved in the first act of disobedience of Adam".[70] But, Hopkins continues, "it is not to be supposed that the offence of Adam is imputed to them to their condemnation, while they are considered as in themselves, in their own persons, innocent; or that they are guilty of the sin of their first father, antecedent to their own sinfulness". All that is meant is that by the aforesaid constitution there is "a certain connection between the first sin of Adam and the sinfulness of his posterity" and by this constitution it had been fixed that "all mankind should sin as Adam had done, and fully consent to his transgression".[71] Thus they joined with him in his transgression and made it their own. This conception of divine constitution appears as a refrain in Hopkins' discussion and upon it the connection of the sin of Adam with the sinfulness of all is made to depend. And, although by reason of this constitution all mankind are born in sin and are sinful from the beginning of their existence, Hopkins defends the constitution as just, wise, and good.

On this analysis of the relation of the sin of Adam to the sin of posterity it must be recognized, however, that *the sin* of Adam is not charged to the account of posterity. In reality there is no imputation of Adam's sin to posterity either *mediately* or *immediately*. Hopkins says expressly, "And if the sinfulness of all the posterity of Adam was certainly connected with his sinning, this does not make them sinners before they actually are sinners; and when they actually become sinners, they themselves are the sinners, it is their

[68] *Works* (Boston, 1854), vol. I, p. 214.
[69] *Ibid.*, pp. 215–217.   [70] *Ibid.*, p. 216.   [71] *Ibid.*, p. 218.

own sin, and they are as blamable and guilty as if Adam had never sinned, and each one were the first sinner that ever existed. The children of Adam are not answerable for his sin, and it is not their sin any further than they approve of it, by sinning as he did. In this way only they become guilty of his sin, viz., by approving of what he did, and joining with him in rebellion. And it being previously certain, by divine constitution, that all mankind would thus sin and join with their common head in rebellion, renders it no less their own sin and crime than if this certainty had taken place on any other ground, or in any other way; or than if there had been no certainty that they would thus all sin, were this possible."[72] The force of this is that posterity is not involved in the sin of Adam by reason of the divinely constituted relationship that exists between Adam and posterity; the divine constitution simply insures that posterity will sin as Adam did.

There are two further observations to be made respecting Hopkins' position. First, the doctrine of mediate imputation as originally formulated laid emphasis upon *hereditary* corruption as the medium through which the first sin of Adam was imputed to posterity. Hopkins is clear to the effect that "mankind are born totally corrupt or sinful, in consequence of the apostasy of Adam"[73] and so "a child, an infant, as soon as he exists, may have moral corruption or sin".[74] But, in view of what has been shown already, this native depravity is not to be construed as the medium through which the sin of Adam is imputed even to infants but only as making it certain that all the members of the race will "begin to sin as soon as they begin to act as moral agents".[75] In this respect also Hopkins can scarcely be classified with the earlier exponents of mediate imputation even though there is a genetic relationship. Secondly, when Hopkins says that the sin, which "takes place in the posterity of Adam, is not properly distinguished into original and actual sin, because it is all really actual, and there is, strictly. speaking, no other sin but actual sin",[76] he is not to be interpreted as equating the word "actual" with what we call "actual transgressions". What he

[72] *Ibid.*, p. 230.   [73] *Ibid.*, p. 226.
[74] *Ibid.*, p. 224.   [75] *Ibid.*, p. 222.   [76] *Ibid.*, p. 224.

means is that whenever sin exists, even in an infant, there is a corrupt inclination that is of the same nature with that which is expressed in overt voluntary transgression. What Hopkins is rightly asserting is that evil inclination always precedes overt sin and that this evil inclination is actually sinful and as evil motion exists in infants. In terms of his own principles, therefore, the sin by which posterity becomes sinful and sins as Adam did is predicable of new born infants by reason of the sinful inclination with which they are born, though they do not yet have the capacity or opportunity for voluntary overt transgression.[77]

In Nathanael Emmons the development of thought which appears in Hopkins takes on a distinctly more advanced complexion. In dealing with the question how we became sinners by Adam, Emmons maintains that "Adam did not make us sinners, by causing us to commit his first offence",[78] nor did Adam transfer to posterity the guilt of his first transgression,[79] and neither did Adam convey to posterity a morally corrupt nature.[80] The only proper answer, in Emmons' esteem, is that since God made Adam the public head of his posterity he "determined to treat them according to his conduct".[81] God suspended the holiness and sinfulness of posterity upon the conduct of Adam and by this divine constitution the whole human race was rendered unholy and depraved because by his first transgression Adam "proved the occasion of God's bringing all his posterity into the world in a state of moral depravity".[82] In Emmons we find the same principle of divine constitution in terms of which all men become sinners but there is not the semblance of the notion that Adam's sin is reckoned to posterity, not even in the form adopted by Hopkins that "they become guilty of his sin . . . by approving of what he did, and joining with him in rebel-

---

[77] Cf. ibid., p. 225. In this respect it appears to me that F. H. Foster's discussion in A Genetic History of the New England Theology (Chicago, 1907), pp. 175 f. is distinctly misleading. He does not discriminate sufficiently to make clear what Hopkins means by "actual" as distinct from volitional action.

[78] Works (Boston, 1842), vol. IV, p. 487.

[79] Ibid., p. 488.   [80] Ibid., p. 490.

[81] Idem.   [82] Ibid., p. 491.

lion". Adam's sin is merely the occasion upon which God acts in accordance with the constitution which he ordained and established.

To much the same effect is the position of Timothy Dwight. *"When I assert, that in consequence of the Apostacy of Adam all men have sinned; I do not intend, that the posterity of Adam is guilty of his transgression.* Moral actions are not, so far as I can see, transferable from one being to another. The personal act of any agent is, in its very nature, the act of that agent solely; and incapable of being participated by any other agent. Of course, the guilt of such a personal act is equally incapable of being transferred, or participated. The guilt is inherent in the action; and is attributable, therefore, to the Agent only. . . . *Neither do I intend, that the descendants of Adam are punished for his transgression."*[83] And Dwight falls back on the same explanation of the universality of sin, namely, that by the state of things that had been constituted all became sinners in consequence of the transgression of Adam.[84]

Even a brief survey of the New England Theology requires the mention of one other in the genealogy, the name of Nathaniel W. Taylor. Taylor, like his predecessors, maintained that *"the sinfulness of mankind is in consequence of the sin of Adam"*.[85] This general proposition, however, does not determine the particular mode of the connection between Adam's sin and the sinfulness of the race. In Taylor's judgment it is in "this general and indefinite manner that the Scriptures exhibit the connection".[86] He protests against what he calls "gratuitous and unauthorized speculation" and proceeds forthwith to two explicit denials: "1. That the posterity of Adam do not become sinners as a consequence of his sin, by being created with a *sinful nature*, or by having such a nature conveyed to them by the laws of propagation. . . . 2. Adam's posterity do not become sinners as a consequence of his sin, *by being guilty of his sin."*[87] These quotations

---

[83] *Theology Explained and Defended* (New York, 1863), vol. I, pp. 478 f.
[84] *Cf. ibid.*, p. 480.
[85] *Essays, Lectures, Etc. upon Select Topics in Revealed Theology* (New York, 1859), p. 242.
[86] *Ibid.*, p. 246.   [87] *Idem.*; *cf.* p. 193.

illustrate Taylor's frank rejection of the doctrine of inherited depravity, as held by the Reformed Churches, and also of the doctrine of the imputation of Adam's sin either in the form of mediate imputation or immediate. Taylor does maintain that *"the constitution or nature"* of mankind is such *"that in all the appropriate or natural circumstances of their existence, they will uniformly sin from the commencement of moral agency"*.[88] In these terms he speaks of total depravity and of mankind as depraved *by nature*. But this is not to be understood in the sense that men are born with a sinful nature or disposition. Nor does it mean that a *sinful* disposition or propensity is the foundation or cause of all sinful volitions. "We mean by depravity", he says, "a sinful volition itself, or rather, a sinful elective preference which becomes predominant in the soul, and comes into existence through that in the physical constitution and in the circumstances of men, which is the ground or reason of the fact. . .".[89] It is for this reason that depravity is *by nature*.

This development of thought in the New England Theology raises a question on which there has been, and on which there will no doubt continue to be, difference of judgment. It is that of the place that Jonathan Edwards occupies in this area of the history of thought. It has been maintained that in his treatise *The Great Christian Doctrine of Original Sin*

[88] *Ibid.*, p. 192; *cf.* also p. 294.

[89] *Ibid.*, p. 204; *cf.* also p. 195: "When I say that mankind are depraved *by nature*, I mean that the depravity which I have already described and proved to pertain to mankind, *is truly and properly traced to the physical or constitutional propensities of man for natural good which belong to man, as a man, in the circumstances of his existence as the cause or occasion of it . . .*".

One further excerpt will help to point up Taylor's position in its divergence from protestant belief and particularly as it is in conflict with the teaching of Jonathan Edwards, the alleged father of this New England Theology. "Nor does the moral depravity of men consist in a sinful nature, which they have corrupted by being *one* with Adam, and by *acting in his act*. To believe that I am one and the same being with another who existed thousands of years before I was born, and that by virtue of this identity I truly acted in his act, and am therefore as truly guilty of his sin as himself, — to believe this, I must renounce the reason which my Maker has given me; I must believe it also, in face of the oath of God to its falsehood, entered upon the record" [Ezek. 18:3, 4] (*Concio ad Clerum*, New Haven, 1828, pp. 5 f.).

Defended he gave expression to the doctrine of the *mediate imputation* of Adam's first sin. In the nineteenth century there were no greater proponents and defenders of the doctrine of immediate imputation than Charles Hodge and William Cunningham and we could scarcely expect any to examine Edwards' discussion with greater care than these two men. Both held that in one chapter of the aforementioned treatise Edwards had given way to the doctrine of mediate imputation. Charles Hodge says: "We think that Edwards here clearly asserts the doctrine of mediate imputation; that is, that the charge of the guilt of Adam's sin is consequent on depravity of heart. . . . The doctrine of Edwards is precisely that which was so formally rejected when presented by Placaeus."[90] Hodge acknowledges, however, that he is not able to reconcile the view set forth by Edwards in that chapter with several passages which occur elsewhere in the same treatise.[91] And William Cunningham likewise says that mediate imputation "was adopted by Jonathan Edwards in his great work on Original Sin. Edwards' views, however, upon this point do not seem to have been clear or consistent, as he sometimes makes statements which manifestly imply or assume the common Calvinistic doctrine."[92]

If Edwards, in the place concerned, gave expression to mediate imputation it would be at least plausible to argue that the development of the New England Theology on this particular question took its point of departure from Edwards and that, though Edwards would have rejected with all his soul the positions espoused by men like Emmons, Dwight, and Taylor, yet Edwards had provided a direction of thought which in due time culminated in these developments. There need be little doubt that the notion of a divine constitution which, as we have seen, plays so large a part in the formulations of Hopkins, Emmons, and Dwight had been derived, proximately at least, from Edwards, and it became in their hands a convenient rubric by which to eliminate altogether the idea of the imputation to posterity of Adam's first sin.

[90] *Op. cit.*, p. 150.
[91] *Ibid.*, p. 151.
[92] *The Reformers and the Theology of the Reformation* (Edinburgh, 1866), p. 384.

Edwards' discussion of the question merits close examination. It is surely significant that so erudite and discriminating a theologian as B. B. Warfield should disagree with Hodge and Cunningham in their assessment of Edwards in this regard. Referring to Edwards he says: "In answering objections to the doctrine of Original Sin, he appeals at one point to Stapfer, and speaks, after him, in the language of that form of doctrine known as 'mediate imputation.' But this is only in order to illustrate his own view that all mankind are one as truly as and by the same kind of divine constitution that an individual life is one in its consecutive moments. Even in this immediate context he does not teach the doctrine of 'mediate imputation,' insisting rather that, Adam and his posterity being in the strictest sense one, in them no less than in him 'the guilt arising from the first existing of a depraved disposition' cannot at all be distinguished from 'the guilt of Adam's first sin'; and elsewhere throughout the treatise he speaks in the terms of the common Calvinistic doctrine."[93] It is the judgment of the present writer that Warfield's interpretation is correct. But since Warfield has not demonstrated his thesis and since the subject deserves more extended treatment it is necessary to show what Edwards' argument really was and how it need not be identified with mediate imputation. Several observations may help to place the question in clearer light.

(i) There need be no doubt that Edwards taught the imputation of Adam's first sin to all of posterity. Some quotations will bear this out conclusively. "That we may proceed with the greater clearness in considering the main objections against supposing the guilt of Adam's sin to be imputed to his posterity; I would premise some observations with a view to the right *stating* of the doctrine of the imputation of Adam's first sin, and then show the *reasonableness* of this doctrine, in opposition to the great clamor raised against it on this head.

"I think it would go far towards directing us to the more clear and distinct conceiving and right stating of this affair,

[93] "Edwards and the New England Theology" in Hastings: *Encyclopaedia of Religion and Ethics* and reprinted in *Studies in Theology* (New York, 1932), p. 530.

were we steadily to bear this in mind, that God, in each step of his proceeding with Adam, in relation to the covenant or constitution established with him, looked on his posterity as being *one with him*. . . . And though he dealt more immediately with Adam, yet it was as the *head* of the whole body, and the *root* of the whole tree; and in his proceedings with him, he dealt with all the branches, as if they had been then existing in their root.

"From which it will follow, that both guilt, or exposedness to punishment, and also depravity of heart, came upon Adam's posterity just as they came upon him, as much as if he and they had all coexisted, like a tree with many branches . . . it is as if, in every step of proceeding, every alteration in the root had been attended, at the same instant, with the same steps and alterations throughout the whole tree, in each individual branch. I think this will naturally follow on the supposition of their being a constituted *oneness* or *identity* of Adam and his posterity in this affair."[94] Again, commenting on Romans 5:12, he says that the latter part of the verse "shows, that in the eye of the Judge of the world, in Adam's first sin, *all* sinned; not only *in some sort*, but all sinned *so* as to be exposed to that *death*, and final destruction, which is the proper *wages of sin*".[95] And referring to the whole passage (Rom. 5:12–19) he says: "As this place in general is very full and plain, so the doctrine of the corruption of nature, as derived from Adam, and also the imputation of his first sin, are *both* clearly taught in it. The *imputation* of Adam's one transgression, is indeed most directly and frequently asserted. We are here assured that *by one man's sin, death passed on all*; all being adjudged to this punishment as having *sinned* (so it is implied) in that one man's sin."[96]

Respecting these quotations two things have to be said. First, the most conclusive evidence in support of a doctrine of mediate imputation would have to be presented if the *prima facie* import of such statements is to be ruled out; the account given is altogether similar to that which we might

[94] *The Great Christian Doctrine of Original Sin Defended* in *Works* (New York, 1855), vol. II, p. 481.
[95] *Ibid.*, p. 459.
[96] *Ibid.*, p. 461; *cf.* p. 460.

expect in an exponent of immediate imputation. If, as Edwards says, God looked on posterity as being one with Adam and looked upon their sin as coexisting with Adam's, then the sin is just as directly theirs as it was his. And this is *immediate* imputation.[97] Secondly, Edwards distinguishes between "the corruption of nature, as derived from Adam" and "the imputation of his first sin". The latter is, therefore, a distinct element and does not consist in the corrupt nature with which we are born. Far less may the imputation of the first sin be said to consist in the approval which we give to Adam's sin by sinning as he did. It is readily seen, therefore, how radically Edwards' view of our relation to the first sin of Adam differs from that of Hopkins. The latter was a student of Edwards but it was not from Edwards he learned that "the children of Adam are not answerable for his sin, and it is not their sin any further than they approve of it, by sinning as he did".

(ii) It is here we encounter, however, the analysis propounded by Edwards which has caused so much difficulty and, in our esteem, misunderstanding, namely, his analysis of the first sin of Adam and of our involvement in it which has been construed as a lapse into the doctrine of mediate imputation. Edwards continues: "Therefore I am humbly of opinion, that if any have supposed the children of Adam to come into the world with a *double guilt*, one the guilt of Adam's sin, another the guilt arising from their having a corrupt heart, they have not well conceived of the matter. The *guilt* a man has upon his soul at his first existence, is one and simple, viz., the guilt of the original apostasy, the guilt of the sin by which the species first rebelled against God. This, and the guilt arising from the first corruption or depraved disposition of the heart, are not to be looked upon as *two* things, *distinctly* imputed and charged upon men in the sight of God. Indeed the guilt that arises from the corruption of the heart, as it remains a confirmed principle, and appears in

---

[97] It is not necessary to discuss the question whether Edwards was a realist in his view of the Adamic union. The realist as well as the federalist holds to *immediate* imputation and the point at issue is not affected by the question of Edwards' affinities on that other issue.

its consequent operations, is a *distinct*, and *additional* guilt: but the guilt arising from the first existing of a depraved disposition in Adam's posterity, I apprehend, is *not* distinct from their guilt of Adam's first sin. For so it was not in Adam himself. The first evil disposition or inclination of the heart of Adam to sin, was not properly distinct from his first act of sin, but was included in it. The external act he committed was no otherwise his, than as his heart was in it, or as that action proceeded from the wicked inclination of his heart. . . . His sin consisted in wickedness of heart, fully sufficient *for*, and entirely amounting *to*, all that appeared in the act he committed."[98] This quotation is pivotal and demands close inspection.

(a) On the face of it this might appear to contradict what has already been maintained that Edwards distinguishes between "the corruption of nature, as derived from Adam" and "the imputation of his first sin". For has he not said that the guilt of Adam's sin and that arising from a corrupt heart are one and not to be looked upon as two things? The solution rests in the distinction which Edwards has been careful to make, namely, the distinction between corruption of the heart as a "confirmed principle" and a corrupt heart as "the first existing of a depraved disposition". If we overlook that distinction and its significance in Edwards' analysis, then we fail to apprehend what is indispensable to a proper understanding of Edwards' position. It is of the latter — "the first existing of a depraved disposition" — and of that *alone* that he speaks when he insists that the first sin of Adam as imputed and the guilt arising from a corrupt heart are one and the same and not two distinct things. To put this beyond dispute we may quote further to show how he labours the distinction. "The depraved disposition of Adam's heart is to be considered two ways. (1) As the first rising of an evil inclination in his heart, exerted in his first act of sin, and the ground of the complete transgression. (2) An evil disposition of heart continuing afterwards, aş a confirmed principle that came by God's forsaking him; which was a *punishment* of his first transgression. This confirmed corruption, by its re-

[98] *Ibid.*, pp. 481 f.

maining and continued operation, brought additional guilt on his soul."[99]

(b) Edwards clearly maintains that the "first existing of a depraved disposition in Adam's posterity", in a word, this "evil disposition" is not a *consequence* of the imputation of the first sin of Adam; it is rather *prior* in the order of nature. "The evil disposition is *first*, and the charge of guilt *consequent*."[100] Now this might appear to be precisely the doctrine of mediate imputation. For is not that doctrine to the effect that the imputation of Adam's sin is mediated through inherited corruption and that the corruption is therefore first in the order of nature and the imputation of Adam's sin the consequence? Verily so. But this latter is not the teaching of Edwards. He says *nothing* of the guilt of Adam's first sin as mediated through hereditary depravity. And this is the all-important difference between Edwards' analysis and that of mediate imputation. When Edwards says that the evil disposition is *first* and the charge of guilt *consequent*, he is not speaking of hereditary depravity and of its relation to the guilt of Adam's first sin. The *evil disposition* which he says is *prior* is that which he constantly insists is *involved in* the first sin of Adam and is really one with it; it is "the guilt of the original apostasy". "The guilt", he says, "arising from the first existing of a depraved disposition in Adam's posterity, I apprehend, is *not* distinct from their guilt of Adam's first sin." This he could not say of *hereditary* depravity. The latter must be identified with what Edwards calls a confirmed and established principle in the heart of posterity and which he says expressly is "a *consequence* and *punishment* of the first apostasy . . . and brings new guilt".[101] What then, we must ask, is this first depraved disposition of the heart which is prior in the order of nature to the imputation of Adam's actual transgression and yet is one with the imputed sin? It is here that Edwards' acumen comes to light.

Edwards' own answer is made perspicuous by his appeal to the analogy of Adam himself as an individual. "The first evil disposition or inclination of the heart of Adam to sin, was

[99] *Ibid.*, p. 482.
[100] *Ibid.*, pp. 482 f.   [101] *Ibid.*, p. 482.

not properly distinct from his first act of sin, but was included in it." He is here reflecting on the simple fact that on exegetical grounds as well as on sound psychological grounds the overt act of sin on Adam's part cannot be conceived of apart from the evil disposition which the overt act registered. It is the biblical truth that Adam was tempted by being drawn away of his own lust and enticed (*cf.* James 1:14, 15). In the order of nature this sinful inclination is prior to the overt act of sin, yet they are one in that the *sin* cannot be construed except in terms of both aspects. All this is so obvious in the case of Adam's own sin, when biblical principles are applied to its analysis, that it is scarcely necessary to labour the point. But the distinctive feature of Edwards' discussion is that in his exposition of the *imputation to posterity* of this first sin of Adam he considered that the sin as *imputed* must be construed as comprising the same two aspects which apply to Adam's own sin. This is to say that if we are to speak of the imputation of Adam's first sin the imputation must include the evil disposition which gave rise to the act committed as well as the act itself. This is what Edwards means by "the first existing of a depraved disposition in Adam's posterity". "The *first existing* of a corrupt disposition in their hearts", he says expressly, "is not to be looked upon as sin belonging to them, *distinct* from their participation of Adam's first sin."[102] This is quite diverse from the notion of mediate imputation. The first existing of the corrupt disposition is just as direct as the participation in Adam's first sin, for the simple reason that it is involved in that participation. And the only antecedent of this participation is "the *union* that the wise author of the world has established between Adam and his posterity" so that God "looked on his posterity as being *one with him*" and "both guilt . . . and also depravity of heart, came upon Adam's posterity just as they came upon him, as much as if he and they had all coexisted, like a tree with many branches".[103]

(c) The evidence would indicate that the depravity remaining as an established and confirmed principle, distinguished by Edwards from the first existing of a depraved disposition, is to be equated with what has generally been called hereditary

[102] *Idem.*
[103] *Ibid.*, pp. 481 f.

depravity. Edwards refers to it in terms of "being born corrupt".[104] He compares this continuance of corruption in the race to the *continued* lack of original righteousness in Adam himself. "But yet, I think it is as truly and in the same manner owing to the course of *nature*, that Adam's posterity came into the world without original righteousness, as that Adam continued without it after he had once lost it."[105] But the most significant observation in this connection is that depravity, viewed in this light, is not only a "*natural* consequence" of the first sin both in Adam and in his posterity but it was also a "*penal* consequence" or punishment of that first sin, a penal consequence or righteous judgment for posterity as it was for Adam himself.[106] This is surely that of which he speaks when he says: "But the depravity of nature remaining an *established principle* in the heart of a child of Adam, and as exhibited in after operations, is a *consequence* and *punishment* of the first apostasy thus participated, and brings new guilt".[107] This is exactly what the proponents of *immediate* imputation have maintained, namely, that hereditary corruption is consequent upon the imputation of the first sin of Adam and is the penal consequence of it. It is only failure to appreciate the distinctions which Edwards makes that will obscure the validity and force of this conclusion. Edwards is plainly on the side of immediate imputation in reference to the relation of hereditary corruption to the first sin of Adam.

(d) When Edwards speaks of "the *derivation of the evil disposition* to the hearts of Adam's posterity" (italics ours)[108] in connection with "the first existing of a depraved disposition", we are not to be misled by the use of the word "derivation" to think that he is referring to derivation by natural generation as in the case of hereditary depravity. After using this term he makes it clear that he prefers to speak of this subject as "the *coexistence* of the evil disposition, implied in Adam's

---

[104] *Cf. ibid.*, p. 480.   [105] *Idem.*

[106] "And just thus I suppose it to be with every natural branch of mankind: all are looked upon as *sinning* in and with their common root; and God righteously withholds special influences and spiritual communications from all, for this sin" (*idem*).

[107] *Ibid.*, p. 482.   [108] *Idem.*

first rebellion".[109] Besides, it had been customary for theologians who espoused immediate imputation to speak of the first sin of Adam as *derived*, when they had no thought of derivation by natural propagation but only by imputation. In fact they can speak of the guilt of Adam's first act of sin as "derived down unto us" by way of imputation and as the ground of the corruption propagated.[110]

(iii) There is one other quotation from Edwards that requires comment. It is that from which, without doubt, a great deal of subsequent formulation in the New England theology has sprung. "The first being of an evil disposition in the heart of a child of Adam, whereby he is disposed to *approve* of the sin of his first father, as fully as he himself approved of it when he committed it, or so far as to imply a full and perfect *consent* of heart to it, I think, is not to be looked upon as a consequence of the imputation of that first sin, any more than the full consent of Adam's own heart, in the act of sinning; which was not consequent on the imputation of his sin to himself, but rather *prior* to it in the order of nature."[111] Edwards is here dealing with the same question of "the first existing of a depraved disposition" in the heart of Adam's posterity which, as has been demonstrated above, he insists is involved in the imputation of Adam's first sin. He is not dealing with the voluntary approval and consent which we may be said to render to Adam's sin when we ourselves come to sin as Adam did; he is dealing with "the first being of an evil disposition in the heart of a child of Adam". This, as well as the whole context, demonstrates that he is explicating the meaning of our direct involvement in the first sin of Adam by reason of the *identity* or *oneness* of Adam and his posterity. He is not by any means alluding to the consequence arising from a divinely established constitution that all men will sin as Adam did. He is saying the opposite, that by the divine constitution there is imputed to posterity the sin of Adam *both as evil disposition and overt action*. Edwards' concept is quite alien to that of Hopkins that when the posterity of Adam

---

[109] *Idem.*

[110] *Cf.* Thomas Goodwin: *Works* (Edinburgh, 1865), vol. X, p. 12; vol. V, p. 182.

[111] Edwards: *op. cit.*, p. 482.

"actually become sinners, they themselves are the sinners, it is their own sin, and they are as blamable and guilty as if Adam had never sinned, and each one were the first sinner that ever existed. The children of Adam are not answerable for his sin, and it is not their sin any further than they approve of it, by sinning as he did."[112] Edwards is dealing with *the disposition* which is an integral element of the sin imputed; Hopkins is dealing with the approval which is given by posterity to the sin of Adam when they sin as he did. Edwards finds this disposition to be an integral aspect of the sin imputed by an analysis of what is involved in Adam's first sin; Hopkins finds that the sin of Adam is not imputed to posterity and that the only way in which Adam's sin may be said to be their sin is that they give their consent to it when they sin after the Adamic pattern. And it is scarcely necessary to remark that it is a far cry from Edwards' insistence, that a depraved disposition is the fountain from which the overt act of sin proceeds and for that reason that the first existing of a depraved disposition is involved for posterity in the imputation of Adam's sin, to the frank disavowal by Taylor of the doctrine "that mankind have a sinful nature which they have corrupted by being one in Adam, and by acting in his act, or sinning in his sin".[113]

There are therefore two conclusions with respect to Edwards. First, the allegation that he propounded the doctrine of mediate imputation rests upon failure to appreciate the precise intent of Edwards' analysis of the first sin of Adam as imputed to posterity. Second, though in some respects the terminology of the other New England theologians mentioned is similar to that of Edwards, on this particular doctrine there is a distinct divergence from the position of Edwards, not only on the part of Emmons, Dwight, and Taylor, but also of Hopkins, and it is not warranted to regard Edwards' teaching on the subject of imputation as providing the first step in the relinquishment and denial of the doctrine of the imputation of Adam's first sin, a denial which became unambiguous in the later developments of this New England Theology. It was

[112] Hopkins: *op. cit.*, p. 230.
[113] Taylor: *Essays* as cited, p. 193.

divergence from Edwards, or at least misunderstanding of his position, that gave birth to this development.[114]

It will have become apparent that the question as to the *mode* by which the sin of Adam comes to be reckoned to posterity must be stated and resolved in terms of the antithesis

[114] J. F. Stapfer, as noted above, has been classified as a proponent of mediate imputation, and Edwards, since he quotes Stapfer with approval (*op. cit.*, pp. 483 f.), is alleged to have followed Stapfer in that regard. If Edwards does not set forth mediate imputation, as has been maintained in the preceding discussion, then Edwards' appeal to Stapfer was not in the interest of mediate imputation. It might still be true, however, that Stapfer cast the thought, which Edwards espoused, in the mould of mediate imputation and Edwards took over the former without the latter. But it is not apparent from a study of Stapfer's reflections on this matter in his *Institutiones Theologiae Polemicae Universae* (Zurich, 1743–1750) that he adopted mediate imputation as opposed to immediate. He says: "Et cum omnes posteri ex primo parente ceu ex radice ortum suum trahunt, generis humani universitas cum stirpe non aliter, quam unicum aliquod totum, sive unica massa considerari potest, ut non sit aliquid a stirpe diversum, et non aliter ab ea differunt posteri ac rami ab arbore.

"Ex quibus facile patet, quomodo stirpe peccante omne illud quod ab ea descendit, et cum ea unicum aliquod totum efficit, etiam peccasse judicari possit, cum a stirpe non differat, sed cum ea unum sit.

"Doctrina de peccati primi parentis imputatione immediata tam incredulos, quam alios offendit, si vero ea, quae hactenus ex ipsis rationis principiis deduximus, perpendantur, facile deprehenditur, S. Litteras nihil hic docere, nisi quod ipsa rei ratio postulat, et justo Dei judicio fieri potuisse, ut primus parens dignus non esset, qui susciperet sobolem sanctam, sed pravam et poenae obnoxiam" (Tom. I, p. 236). This is intended to be a defence of immediate imputation. And when, in subsequent sections of his *Institutes*, he enters into more detail (Tom. IV, pp. 513 f.; 561–564) there does not appear to be evidence of mediate imputation. In answer to the objection urged against the imputation of Adam's sin that we never committed the same sin with Adam he draws the distinction between the physical act and the morality of the act and pleads that it is in respect of the latter only that posterity committed the same sin, that is to say, are to be "looked upon as having committed, in a moral estimation, the same sin or transgression of the law in number and in kind" (*ibid.*, p. 514). And when Stapfer contends that the imputation of Adam's first sin must never be conceived of in abstraction from our native corruption and calls the latter *mediate* imputation in distinction from the guilt of Adam's sin as *immediate*, there is no proof of a position identical with or tending to mediate imputation (*ibid.* pp. 562 f.). Stapfer cannot in this case be shown to do more than was characteristic of earlier Reformed theologians, namely, to insist that the sin of Adam as imputed and hereditary depravity must not be separated or conceived of in abstraction from each other.

between mediate and immediate imputation as that antithesis had been sharply defined in the Placaean debate of the seventeenth century. The developments of the New England Theology from Samuel Hopkins onwards gave a new direction to thought on the subject of the relation of posterity to the sin of Adam, and so radical was the divergence that this New England Theology cannot properly be characterized as a doctrine of *mediate imputation*. However important these developments were and however much they must be taken into account in dealing with the whole question of the effect upon posterity of Adam's sin, yet in a discussion of the precise question as it was formulated in the debates of the seventeenth century the New England Theology does not contribute anything to elucidate or defend the doctrine of mediate imputation. These New England theologians did reject immediate imputation. In that respect they were at one with the exponents of mediate imputation. It may be that their rejection of immediate imputation logically involved the rejection also of mediate imputation and they were consistent in bringing to a logical issue what is implicit in the denial of the doctrine of immediate imputation. In that event the New England development of thought brought to its logical result what was inherent in the classic doctrine of mediate imputation as propounded by Placaeus. But our concern is not with the logical consequences which proceed from the doctrine of mediate imputation but with this doctrine itself as it was understood and propounded by its representative proponents. Mediate imputation does maintain that the sin of Adam was imputed to posterity, that posterity was involved in Adam's sin, and that the sin of the one man Adam was the sin of all. And the question is whether this involvement is *directly* based upon the relation which Adam sustained to posterity or whether it is mediated through the inheritance from Adam of a corrupt nature. It is with that restricted question in view that we turn to the exegetical data.

2. *Immediate Imputation.*

It is assumed on the basis of earlier study in this series that the only feasible interpretation of Romans 5:12–19 is to the effect that the one trespass of Adam is the sin of all, that when

Paul says "one sinned" and "all sinned" he refers to the same sin viewed in its twofold aspect as the sin of Adam, the one man, and the sin of all his posterity. Our question now is simply whether there are any considerations in this passage, or others, which bear on the mode of imputation. Is it mediate or immediate? It is well to have the question sharply focused: does the evidence indicate that the sin of Adam is reckoned as the sin of all through the medium of inherited depravity? Or does the evidence point to the immediacy of conjunction which the doctrine of immediate imputation has maintained? The following propositions, it will surely be granted, are germane to the question at issue, and, if they are shown to be well grounded, they determine the question.

(i) *The immediate conjunction of the sin of Adam and the death of all.* Romans 5:12, 15, 17, furnish the basis for this inference.

In verse 12 the particular point of significance for our present interest is the force of καὶ οὕτως in the middle of the verse. It is, as shown earlier, coordinative and continuative. But in οὕτως there is the note of comparison, though not the kind of comparison that would supply the apodosis to ὥσπερ at the beginning of the verse. What then is this comparison? In the first two clauses reference is made to the sin of Adam and to the death which was its consequence. Summarily the thought is: Adam sinned and he died. In the case of the individual, Adam, we may not interject any medium between his sin and the death inflicted upon him. No other sin than that which the apostle refers to repeatedly as the one sin of the one man Adam needs to be intruded to explain or validate the death of Adam. Furthermore, it would be alien to the sustained thought of the whole passage to intrude any other aspect of Adam's sinfulness as the ground of his death. Far less would it be consonant with the passage to think of Adam's subsequent depravity as the medium through which death came to lay its hold upon him. This is just saying that here there is an immediate juxtaposition of Adam's sin and the death that followed. Now the force of καὶ οὕτως, introducing the next two clauses, is to institute a parallelism. Just as sin and death entered with Adam, so sin and death became the lot of all men: Adam sinned and he died — there is immediate conjunction. All sinned (in Adam, as argued already) and they died — there is the same immediate conjunction. It would be just as arbitrary and indefensible to interject the thought of mediating depravity in the latter case as it would be in the case of Adam himself. To suppose that any other factor is interposed between the involvement of all in the sin of Adam and the death of all that results would interfere with the analogy expressed in οὕτως. And the conclusion to which we are driven is that when Paul says "death penetrated to all men" it is quite contrary to the terms of verse 12, as well as of the entire passage, to think of inherited depravity as the medium through which the death contemplated is conceived of as penetrating to all. But if mediate imputation is correct this is what must be done. For if inherited depravity mediates the imputation of Adam's sin it must also mediate the death which is its consequence. In verse 12 it is impossible to interject any other consideration as the reason for the death of all than the one sin of Adam in which all are regarded by the apostle as involved.

In verse 15 — "by the trespass of the one the many died" — the death of all is brought into immediate conjunction with the one sin of Adam. This scarcely needs argument. The supposition that inherited depravity intervenes as the medium through which the trespass of the one man takes its effect would contradict Paul's emphasis. For, in that event, we should have to suppose that posterity is reckoned as sinful and therefore as inflicted with death before the sin of Adam is imputed and takes its effect. But what Paul is saying is that it is by the trespass of the one that the many died, and if this does not have the priority, if the trespass of the one and the death of the many do not stand in such close relationship that they are self-explanatory, then the patent purpose and emphasis of the apostle break down.

In verse 17 — "by the trespass of the one death reigned through the one" — we are again confronted with the one sin of Adam as the explanation of the universal reign of death. And even more pointedly, perhaps, than in verse 15 do we detect how alien to the conjunction which the apostle is so intent upon asserting is the intrusion of hereditary depravity between "the trespass of the one" and the reign of death through the one. The conjunction is of the kind that comports only with the doctrine of immediate imputation.

(ii) *The immediate conjunction of the sin of Adam and the condemnation of all.* This appears from verses 16 and 18.

When the apostle says in verse 16 that "the judgment was *from one* unto condemnation" it is not immediately apparent whether he means the one man Adam or the one sin of Adam. In the preceding clause δι' ἑνὸς ἁμαρτήσαντος refers to Adam as having sinned and it could be that the ἐξ ἑνός of the next clause has in view the one man Adam rather than the one trespass of Adam. But the contrast drawn in the second and third clauses would distinctly favour the view that ἐξ ἑνός refers to the one trespass. For ἐξ ἑνός is contrasted with ἐκ πολλῶν παραπτωμάτων — "from many trespasses" — and one trespass can more suitably be contrasted with many trespasses than can one man. But even if we allow doubt to remain as to the reference of ἐξ ἑνός in verse 16 there can be no doubt as to the import of verse 18. There it is explicitly stated that "through one trespass" — δι' ἑνὸς παραπτώματος — judgment came "upon all men unto condemnation" This is an unambiguous assertion to the effect that the ground, or, if we will, the medium, of the condemnation of all is the one trespass of Adam. To intrude the medium of inherited depravity would introduce another factor, namely, another sin or aspect of sinfulness, which would plainly violate the emphasis that it was from the *one trespass* that the judgment of condemnation came upon all. In other words, the interjection of inherited depravity, which, on the premises of mediate imputation, is the crucial and explanatory consideration, posits an addition which is palpably inconsistent with the apostle's emphasis upon the singularity of the trespass from which universal condemnation proceeded. This is just saying that no other sin or aspect of sinfulness can be allowed to interfere with the conjunction of the one trespass of Adam and the condemnation of all. And this means immediate conjunction. If we may return to verse 16, it is therefore Paul's doctrine that the judgment was from one trespass unto condemnation whether this is what he expressly says in verse 16 or not. And even if we suppose that the ἐξ ἑνός of verse 16 refers to Adam (as is not probable for the reason mentioned above) rather than to the one trespass, we must remember that it is Adam *as sinning* who is in view, namely, the δι' ἑνὸς ἁμαρτήσαντος of the preceding clause, and the *sinning* contemplated can be none other than the one trespass of verses 15 and 18. Hence the express or clearly implied thought of verse 16 is that the condemnation of all proceeded from the one trespass of Adam and the same kind of conjunction appears in verse 16 as is unmistakable in verse 18. It is immediate imputation, therefore, that verses 16 and 18 establish in respect of the *modus operandi* of universal condemnation.

Since then we have found that both death and condemnation are immediately grounded upon the one trespass of Adam, we would have to infer that the sin of Adam would in like manner be brought into immediate conjunction with the sin of all. But the apostle does not leave this climactic feature of his doctrine to good and necessary inference. He deals with it expressly.

(iii) *The immediate conjunction of the sin of Adam and the sin of all.* This is apparent from verses 12 and 19.

In verse 12 Paul says, "all sinned". We found already that this is but another aspect from which the one sin of the one man Adam may be viewed. The one explanation of this twofold aspect from which the sin of Adam may be viewed is the solidarity existing between Adam and his posterity. Pertinent to our present question, the intrusion of hereditary depravity as a mediating instrument is entirely unnecessary once we recognise the fact of solidarity. And, besides, hereditary depravity as an explanation is not only unnecessary; it would also be extraneous and disturbing. Hereditary depravity emanates from the solidarity; it is a process subsequent to the solidarity. It is therefore the solidarity itself and not a process emanating from it that adequately and suitably explains the "all sinned" of verse 12. Verse 19, however, puts the thesis in clearer focus. "Through the disobedience of the one man the many were constituted sinners." When the apostle says, "constituted sinners" he has surely in mind that which is logically first in our becoming or being reckoned sinners. And when we ask: how were men thus constituted? The answer is at hand; it was "through the disobedience of the one man". In terms of the context it is the one trespass of the one man Adam. Mediate imputation asserts that what is basically and logically first in constituting men sinners is hereditary depravity and not the disobedience of the one man. The same kind of incompatibility appears at this point as we noted already in connection with death and condemnation. Paul brings the sin of all into direct relation to the sin of Adam; mediate imputation denies this conjunction and the contradiction is overt. In Paul's thought not only is death inflicted upon all by the *one trespass* of Adam, not only is condemnation pronounced upon all by this *one trespass*, but by that same trespass, in verse 19 called disobedience, all are constituted sinners. As we contemplate the sin, condemnation, and death of all, in other words the universal reign of sin, condemnation, and death, we have nothing in this passage to provide the explanation but the one sin of Adam. These two facts are brought into direct relation to each other. And the only consideration left for inference on our part is that they stand in this relationship to each other because there is the solidarity of the race in the sin of Adam. Paul leaves no room for any other factor or constitution.

These conclusions may be correlated with what is implicit in I Corinthians 15:22: "In Adam all die". That death is the wages of sin (Rom. 6:23) and that death cannot be conceived of as existing or as exercising its sway apart from sin is the Pauline principle. When he says that "in Adam all die" it is impossible, on Pauline premises, to exclude the antecedence of sin and the only way in which the antecedence in this case could obtain is that all are conceived of as having sinned in Adam. Otherwise the statement "in Adam all die" would be without the foundation which Paul's principles demand. As we correlate this premise of I Corinthians 15:22, namely, that "in Adam all sinned", with the teaching of Romans 5:12–19 there is only one conclusion: all sinned in Adam in his one trespass. And the immediacy of conjunction established by so many distinct lines of argument from Romans 5:12–19 is the same kind of conjunction which suits the proposition presupposed in I Corinthians 15:22 and, in reality, is the kind of conjunction which the proposition would naturally be understood to imply.

(iv) *The analogy supports immediate imputation.* The parallel instituted in Romans 5:12–19 as a whole is that between the way in which condemnation passes upon men through the sin of Adam and the way justification comes to men through the righteousness of Christ. In the case of the righteousness of Christ (designated δικαίωμα in verse 18 and ὑπακοή in verse 19) this righteousness comes to the justified through no other medium than that of union with Christ; it is not mediated through the righteousness inwrought in the believer in regeneration and sanctification. To use the language of imputation, it is not by mediate imputation that believers come into the possession of the righteousness of Christ in justification. It would be contradictory of Paul's doctrine of justification to suppose that the righteousness and obedience of Christ become ours unto justification *because* holiness is conveyed to us from Christ or that the righteousness of Christ is mediated to us through the holiness generated in us by regeneration. The one ground upon which the imputation of the righteousness of Christ becomes ours is the union with Christ. In other words, the justified person is constituted righteous by the obedience of Christ because of the solidarity established between Christ and the justified person. The solidarity constitutes the bond by which the righteousness of Christ becomes that of the believer. Once the solidarity is posited there is no other mediating factor that could be conceived of as necessary to the conjunction of the righteousness of Christ and the righteousness of the believer. This is to say that the conjunction is immediate. If the case is thus on that side of the analogy which pertains to justification, we should expect the *modus operandi* to be the same in connection with condemnation. To put the argument in the order underlying the parallelism, immediate imputation in the case of Adam's sin provides the parallel by which to illustrate the doctrine of justification and is thus eminently germane to the governing thesis of the apostle in this part of the epistle.

CHAPTER FOUR

IN these studies we have been concerned with the subject of the relation which Adam as the first man sustained to the members of the human race and, more particularly, with the relation which the members of the race sustain to the first sin of Adam. The various aspects of the subject already discussed lead up to the concluding question: what is the character of the involvement on the part of posterity in Adam's trespass? In terms of *sin* what was entailed for posterity? If all sinned in Adam, how are we to define this sin of all in the sin of Adam?

V. The Sin Imputed

When we speak of the sin of Adam as imputed to posterity, it is admitted that nowhere in Scripture is our relation to the trespass of Adam expressly defined in terms of imputation. And since this is the case the biblical teaching respecting the involvement of the race in the first sin of Adam must not be prejudiced or distorted by the use of the term "imputation" if it does not adequately or accurately convey the biblical meaning. The word has been widely used, however, in this connection and there is no good reason for abandoning its use. The Scripture does employ the notion of imputation with reference to the judgment which God entertains and registers in the case of the person who has sinned or is a sinner. This is true in both Testaments (*cf.* Lev. 17:4; Psalm 32:2; Rom. 4:8; II Cor. 5:19). The negative expressions to the effect that God does not impute sin to those whose sins are forgiven imply that God does impute sin and that the blessedness of forgiveness consists in the reversal of this imputation. We may not forget, furthermore, that even in the passage with which we are particularly concerned the idea of imputation is clearly enunciated. "Sin is not imputed when there is no law" (Rom. 5:13), implying, of course, that sin is imputed wherever the transgression of law obtains. Hence the judgment of God with reference to sin can be scripturally stated by saying that God imputes sin, and this means that he reckons the sinner to be guilty of the sin which belongs to him or is committed by him. If we say that the trespass of Adam is imputed to posterity, all we can strictly and properly be regarded as meaning is that the sin of Adam is reckoned by God as the sin also of posterity. The same sin is laid to their account; it is reckoned as theirs. We may not allow any arbitrary associations which may be attached to the word "imputation" to perplex or obscure this simple meaning of the term "impute". If it is applied in its scriptural import to the relation we sustain to Adam's sin, it means simply that this sin is reckoned by God as our sin. We have already found that the teaching of Paul is to the effect that the trespass of the one was the sin of all, that when Adam sinned all sinned. If all sinned in Adam, it is esteemed by God to be so; it is judged by God for what it is. Nothing less or more is meant by the imputation of Adam's sin to posterity. And if we restrict ourselves to the biblical notion of imputation, the use of the term throws no more light upon the questions that arise and which we proceed to discuss than do these other synonymous expressions. In other words, we may not think that the term "imputation" itself possesses some differentiating notion that supplies the solution to the question of the precise character of our involvement in the sin of Adam. So our question now is: what was reckoned in the divine judgment as having occurred in the case of posterity when Adam fell? God's judgment is always according to truth, and what he reckoned as having occurred did actually occur. The question is then: what did happen? And this is to say, what was imputed to posterity?

Perhaps we can discover the *status quaestionis* if we consider, first of all, the rather emphatic position taken by Charles Hodge. In the nineteenth century no one entered the lists in defence of the doctrine of immediate imputation more vigorously than Dr. Hodge. In dealing with the question of that which was imputed to posterity he says: "As he (Adam)

fell from the estate in which he was created, they (posterity)
fell with him in his first transgression, so that the penalty of
that sin came upon them as well as upon him. Men therefore
stood their probation in Adam. As he sinned, his posterity
came into the world in a state of sin and condemnation."[115]
This would rather clearly amount to the assertion that
posterity sinned and fell in Adam. In his commentary on
the epistle to the Romans there is repeated use of such formulae as these: that "all sinned when Adam sinned", that
they "were regarded and treated as sinners on account of
his sin",[116] that by the sin of Adam all "were set down in the
rank or category of sinners".[117] Thus there can be no question
but Dr. Hodge would affirm that all sinned in Adam and fell
with him in his first transgression. However, when Hodge
explicates this statement he is also insistent that this sin of
posterity or, in other words, the sin of Adam imputed to
posterity consists simply in *the obligation to satisfy justice.*
"To impute", he says, "is to reckon to, or to lay to one's
account. . . . To impute sin, in Scriptural and theological
language, is to impute the guilt of sin. And by guilt is not
meant criminality or moral ill-desert, or demerit, much less
moral pollution, but the judicial obligation to satisfy justice."[118] Since Dr. Hodge elsewhere elaborates on this question

---

[115] *Systematic Theology*, vol. II, p. 196.

[116] *Commentary on the Epistle to the Romans* (Edinburgh, 1864), p. 151.

[117] *Ibid.*, p. 173; *cf.* also *Essays and Reviews* (New York, 1857), pp.
49 ff., in which we find repeatedly such formulae as the following: "all
men are regarded and treated as sinners, on account of Adam's sin"
(p. 60); "we are treated as sinners on his account, or, in other words, have
his sin put to our account" (p. 82; *cf.* pp. 61, 63, 79, 81).

[118] *Systematic Theology*, II, p. 194. William Cunningham might be
quoted to a similar effect. "The peculiarity of the doctrine of imputation,
as generally held by Calvinistic divines, is, that it brings in *another* species
of oneness or identity as subsisting between Adam and his posterity . . . so
that, while there was no *actual* participation by them in the moral culp-
ability or blameworthiness of his sin, they became, in consequence of
his failure to fulfil the covenant engagement, *rei*, or incurred *reatus*, or
guilt in the sense of legal answerableness, to this effect, that God, on the
ground of the covenant, regarded and treated them as if they had themselves been guilty of the sin whereby the covenant was broken; and that
in this way they became involved in all the natural and penal consequences
which Adam brought *upon himself* by his first sin" (*Historical Theology*,

in the most polemic fashion,[119] we are not left in any doubt —
he conceived of the imputation of Adam's sin to posterity as
consisting in the obligation to satisfy justice. The involvement
of the race in the sin of Adam is, therefore, to be interpreted
in these restricted terms and the imputation to posterity is
to be equated with the obligation to satisfy justice. To use
the Latin terms, the imputation was not the *culpa* of Adam's
sin, nor the *demeritum*, but simply the *reatus*, specifically the
reatus poenae.

Dr. Hodge in his polemic for this interpretation of the
import of imputation could enlist and appeal to the statements
of others in the Reformed tradition. He quotes, for example,
from John Owen who does say quite plainly that "nothing is
intended by the imputation of sin unto any, but the rendering
of them justly obnoxious unto the punishment due unto that
sin".[120] There are, however, questions that arise in connection
with this equation. The first is one of exegesis. Are we
justified in interpreting the pivotal expressions "all sinned"
and "the many were constituted sinners" (Rom. 5:12, 19)
in this restricted sense, namely, "were placed under the
obligation to satisfy justice"?

There is, of course, no question but the imputation of sin
carries with it the *reatus*, the obligation to satisfy justice.
But we may not overlook the fact that Paul in Romans 5:12–19
uses not only expressions which imply the penal consequence
of sin but also the expressions which imply involvement in
sin itself. As has been observed repeatedly in other connections in the course of this study, Paul not only takes account
of *death* as penetrating to all and as reigning over all by
means of the one trespass (vss. 12, 14, 15, 17) and not only of

Edinburgh, 1870, vol. I, p. 515). *Cf.*, also, Thomas Ridgeley: *A Body of
Divinity* (New York, 1855), vol. I, p. 406.

[119] *Cf. Theological Essays: Reprinted from the Princeton Review* (New
York and London, 1846), pp. 128–217. "And if there is anything in which
Calvinists are agreed, it is in saying that when they affirm 'that the guilt of
Adam's sin has come upon us,' they mean, exposure to punishment on
account of that sin" (p. 140; *cf. passim* where this thesis is presented and
argued *in extenso*).

[120] John Owen: *The Doctrine of Justification by Faith, Works*, ed. Goold
(Edinburgh, 1862), vol. V, p. 324; ed. Russell (London, 1826), vol. XI,
p. 400.

condemnation as coming upon all through the one trespass, but also of the fact that all were constituted *sinners*. That is to say, not only does the wages of sin come upon all, not only does the judgment of condemnation pass upon all, but all are indicted with the sin which is the basis of condemnatory judgment and of which death is the wages. If the imputation referred to in verse 13 meant merely the obligation to satisfy justice, the *reatus poenae*, then it would have sufficed for Paul to speak of death and condemnation. In reality he is not content with the thought of penal consequence; he lays the foundation for all predication in terms of consequence in the propositions, "all sinned", "the many were constituted sinners" (vss. 12, 19), and, by implication, "sin was imputed to all" (vs. 13). It is this distinct progression of thought that prevents us from taking for granted that propositions to the effect that "all sinned" or were "constituted sinners" may be interpreted to mean simply, "were placed under the sentence of condemnation" or "were made judicially liable to the sanctions of justice".

It is true that there are expressions in the Old Testament in which the term for sin is used in the sense of being counted as a sinner. To these Dr. Hodge appeals (Gen. 43:9; 44:32; I Kings 1:21) and concludes, "To sin, therefore, or to be a sinner may, in Scriptural language, mean *to be counted an offender*, that is, to be regarded and treated as such".[121] But it is not apparent that these texts mean simply to be liable to the punishment which the respective situations contemplated, and we may not assume that to be counted a sinner, in the usage of Scripture or theology, may be reduced to the notion of obligation to satisfy justice. Furthermore, though it were conceded that "visiting the iniquity of the fathers upon the children" (Exod. 20:5; 34:7; Numb. 14:18; *cf.* Jer. 32:18; Lam. 5:7) refers to no more than bearing the penalty of the sins of the fathers, we may not conclude that no more is implied in the Pauline expressions of Romans 5:12, 13, 19 than that posterity is subject to the punishment of Adam's sin.[122] To say the least, therefore, we are placed under

---

[121] *Commentary* as cited, p. 152.
[122] *Cf.* Hodge's discussion in *Theological Essays*, pp. 153 f.

the necessity of exercising caution and hesitation before we grant that the terms "sinned" and "were constituted sinners" (Rom. 5:12, 19) are to be construed as merely denoting *the obligation to satisfy justice.*

There is another consideration derived from the parallel which the apostle institutes in this passage which should arouse suspicion as to the adequacy of the formula which Hodge employs. The parallel to the imputation of Adam's sin is the imputation of Christ's righteousness. Or, to use Paul's own terms, being "constituted sinners" through the disobedience of Adam is parallel to being "constituted righteous" through the obedience of Christ. In justification, according to Reformed theology and Dr. Hodge's own position, it is not merely the *judicial benefit* of Christ's righteousness or obedience that is imputed to believers but the righteousness itself. It would be to evacuate Paul's doctrine of justification of its most precious and central significance to reduce the imputation to the judicial consequence. The judicial consequence flows from the imputation of the righteousness itself, and the two may not be equated. We should expect this same distinction and sequence to obtain on the other side of the parallel, namely, the imputation of Adam's sin. And it is the same kind of distinction that the Pauline expressions bear out.

It is beside the point at the present stage of our discussion to appeal to the fact that we are not made subjectively and morally righteous by the imputation of the obedience of Christ. For the question now is whether our being constituted righteous through the obedience of Christ involves more than the judicial consequence of that constituting act and whether the latter is but the result of an antecedent fact which must, in the nature of the case, be distinguished from the judicial consequence. The only observation necessary at this stage is that there is surely room for a concept of being "constituted righteous" other than that of being made subjectively and morally righteous, a concept which falls into the category of forensic relationship and one that is not to be explicated in terms merely of the corresponding award or consequence. And, in like manner, we must leave room for a concept of being "constituted sinners" that is antecedent to our obligation to satisfy justice and may not be reduced, in its definition, to this resulting obligation.

It can readily be understood why Dr. Hodge in his vigorous defence of the doctrine of immediate imputation should have defined imputation as consisting in the obligation to satisfy justice. He was confronted with the objection that immediate imputation involved the notion that thereby we are represented as *personally* and *voluntarily* participating in the first sin of Adam. And to such a supposition there is the obvious objection that when Adam sinned we, his posterity, did not exist as personal voluntary agents and could not be conceived of as acting thus personally and voluntarily. Furthermore, he was required to deal with the objection that immediate imputation supposed the transfer of moral character from Adam to posterity. He was emphatic in his denial of any such implication on the ground, with which his opponents agreed, that the moral quality of an action cannot be transferred from the perpetrator to another who is not the actual perpetrator. Denying, therefore, both of these allegations with respect to the import of immediate imputation he was under the necessity of defining the imputation in terms which would patently steer clear of both of these notions. The concept which appeared to him to define this differentiation and at the same time conform to biblical teaching was that of *reatus*, the obligation to satisfy justice.

There was also another reason why Dr. Hodge was so jealous for this defining concept. It is the analogy between the imputation of Adam's sin to posterity and the imputation of our sins to Christ in his vicarious sin-bearing. This argument appears again and again in his polemics. One quotation will suffice. "When it is said that our sins were imputed to Christ, or that He bore our sins, it is not meant that he actually committed our sins, or that He was morally criminal on account of them, or that the demerit of them rested upon Him . . . . And when it is said that the sin of Adam is imputed to his posterity, it is not meant that they committed his sin, or were the agents of his act, nor is it meant that they are morally criminal for his transgression . . . but simply that . . . his sin is the judicial ground of the condemnation of his race."[123]

The question remains, however, whether Dr. Hodge, in guarding against misunderstanding and misrepresentation of the doctrine of immediate imputation, has done justice to the biblical data and in his zeal for sharp differentiation between imputation, on the one hand, and personal participation or transfer of moral character, on the other, has not oversimplified the problem and left out of account a certain implicate of our relation to Adam's sin, enunciated, for example, in Paul's expression "constituted sinners" (Rom. 5:19). And there is also the question whether the analogy of the vicarious sin-bearing of Christ provides a basis for the precise inference which Dr. Hodge elicits from it. After all, there is a uniqueness to Christ's sin-bearing, and while there is undoubtedly analogy it may well be that we shall have to discover discrimination at the point where Dr. Hodge insists upon identity.

In connection with Hodge's insistence that the obligation to satisfy justice defines for us what is involved in the imputation to posterity of Adam's sin, there is not only the question of exegesis; there is also the question as to whether Hodge's position adequately represents the thought of Reformed theologians and, more particularly, the thought of those who have been the exponents of immediate imputation. It must be admitted that this is not a simple question. There is particularly the difficulty connected with the precise import of the word "guilt" as used in this connection. And of considerable importance is the definition of the Latin term *reatus* and its relations to *culpa*, on the one hand, and *poena*, on the other.

If we examine the teaching of John Owen to whom, for example, Hodge made appeal, we shall find that certain positions taken by Owen in his exposition of imputation would appear, at least, to be considerably different from those of Dr. Hodge. The quotation already given from Owen accords with the insistence of Hodge that the guilt imputed to posterity is the obligation to satisfy justice. More might be quoted from Owen along this line. However, in the context of that same quotation Owen also says: "But that men should be liable unto death, which is nothing but the punishment of sin, when they have not sinned, is an open contradiction. For although God, by his sovereign power, might inflict death on an innocent creature, yet that an innocent creature should be guilty of death is impossible: for to be guilty of death, is to have sinned. Wherefore this expression, 'Inasmuch as all have sinned,' expressing the desert and guilt of death then when sin and death first entered into the world, no sin can be intended in it but the sin of Adam, and our interest therein: 'Eramus enim omnes ille unus homo;' and this can be no otherwise but by the imputation of the guilt of that sin unto us."[124] The thought to be noted here is the insistence that there can be no obligation to the penalty of sin without the sin which is the proper ground of that obligation. This means that the obligation to penalty cannot obtain unless there is antecedent sin. And surely this implies that the imputation of Adam's sin to us cannot be defined in terms of the obligation to penalty; the latter is the effect of the imputation. Again, in reference to the distinction between *culpa* and *poena*, Owen says: "Much less is there any thing of weight in the distinction of 'reatus culpae' and 'reatus poenae;' for this 'reatus culpae' is nothing but 'dignitas poenae propter culpam' .... So, therefore, there can be no punishment, nor 'reatus poenae,' the guilt of it, but where there is 'reatus culpae,' or sin considered with its guilt. . ."[125] This latter quotation conveniently introduces us to what may well be considered as the consensus of Reformed theologians of the sixteenth and seventeenth centuries.

Owen's rejection of the distinction between *reatus culpae* and *reatus poenae* reflects a widespread antipathy to this distinction among protestant theologians. This antipathy sprang from recoil against the Romish abuse of the distinction by which a foundation was laid for the doctrine of penitential and purgatorial satisfaction — in the pardon of sin the *culpa* is remitted but for the temporal *poena* of post-baptismal sins

[124] *Works*, ed. Goold, V, p. 325; ed. Russell, XI, p. 401.
[125] *Ibid.*, V, p. 199; XI, p. 247.

satisfaction must be made either in this life or in purgatory.[126] But of more importance for the subject in hand is the way in which Reformed theologians conceived of the relations of *culpa*, *reatus*, and *poena* and, most particularly, their insistence that there can be no *poena* or, for that matter, no *reatus poenae* apart from *culpa*.

On the relations of these three elements, the definition of Van Mastricht is representative and, in any event, most succinct: "*Reatus* is therefore the *medium quid* between *culpa* and *poena*, for it arises from *culpa* and leads to *poena*, so that it is at the same time the *reatus* of *culpa* and of *poena* and, as a medium, intervenes between these two termini and takes its name from both equally".[127] *Reatus* is therefore the liability in punishment arising from the *culpa* which sin entails. While it is not improper to speak of the *reatus culpae*, yet this may not be thought of as a *reatus* distinct from *reatus poenae* for, in reality, the *reatus culpae* is simply the *reatus poenae*. In our terms, the liability entailed in blameworthiness is nothing other than the obligation to penalty, the obligation to satisfy justice. We should expect from this definition of the relations of *culpa*, *reatus*, and *poena* that *reatus poenae* could not be conceived of apart from *culpa*. But the Reformed theologians have been very jealous to insist upon this principle and it is not superfluous to cite some of the copious evidence which the Reformed theology furnishes in support of this principle.

---

[126] *Cf.* Francis Turretine: *Institutio Theologiae Elencticae*, Loc. IX, Quaest. III, §VI; M. Leidecker: *Medulla Theologica*, Cap. IX, §XV (Utrecht, 1683, pp. 150 f.). James Henley Thornwell, though rejecting the Romish doctrine, defends the propriety of the distinction and maintains that it is really the distinction, which Protestant theologians made, between *reatus potentialis* and *reatus actualis*, the former being the intrinsic demerit and the latter that arising from the ordination of God; *cf. Collected Writings*, vol. I, p. 423.

[127] *Theoretico-Practica Theologia*, Lib. IV, Cap. II, §VII (Amsterdam, 1724, Tom. I, p. 444). To the same effect is the formulation of the *Synopsis Purioris Theologiae*, known as the Leyden Synopsis, which reads: "Primum est *Reatus*, quo nomine intelligitur obligatio ad poenam, sive vinculum illud inter peccatum et poenam, quasi medium interjectum, quo peccator ad subeundam poenam, et quamdiu durat reatus, ad poenae quam subit, durationem, arctissime obligatur" (Disp. XV, §XXXVII).

The principle in question is clearly enunciated in Calvin. In the first few chapters of the second book of the *Institutes* he is dealing specifically with the subject of original sin and hereditary depravity, and it is in this connection that he gives expression to the axiom concerned. Yet it is stated as a principle that holds true in general. Of the original sin with which infants are afflicted he says: "Whence it follows that it is properly accounted sin in the sight of God because there is no *reatus* without *culpa*".[128] This is to say that there is no liability to penalty without blameworthiness. From this, as a general principle, he argues for the sinfulness of the depravity with which infants are born.

Jerome Zanchius, in dealing with the imputation to us of the disobedience of Adam, is explicit. His words are: "We therefore say that this disobedience, although it could not pass to us as act, nevertheless did pass to us as *culpa* and *reatus* through imputation, inasmuch as that sin of Adam as our head God imputes to us, and that most justly, as the members".[129] Again, "the disobedience of Adam comes upon us as *culpa* and *reatus*".[130]

The Leyden Synopsis is equally explicit when it says: "The form of original sin consists in that transgression and disobedience by which all who were in Adam . . . sinned with him; the disobedience and *culpa* with its resulting *reatus* were justly imputed by God as judge to all the sons of Adam, inasmuch as they all were and are one with him".[131]

Although Amesius does not make use of the term *culpa* in this connection, yet it is of interest to note the terms in which he speaks of imputation and how he distinguishes between imputation and the communication that takes place through natural generation. "This propagation of sin consists of two parts, namely, imputation and real communication.

"By imputation the same singular act of disobedience, which was Adam's, becomes also ours.

---

[128] "Unde sequitur, proprie coram Deo censeri peccatum quia non esset reatus absque culpa" (*Inst.*, II, i, 8).
[129] *Opera Theologica*, 1613, Tom. IV, col. 36.
[130] *Ibid.*, col. 38; *cf.* also coll. 39, 41.
[131] Disp. XV, §XXIV.

"By real communication the same singular sin is not derived to us, but the same in kind or of like reason and nature."[132] Turretine, also, affirms the same principle in at least two different connections. In reflecting on the falsity of the Romish distinction between *reatus culpae* and *reatus poenae* he says that "the vanity of the distinction is apparent from the nature of both; for since *culpa* and *poena* are related and *reatus* is nothing else than obligation to *poena*, which springs from *culpa*, they both stand or fall together, so that if *culpa* is removed and with it its *reatus* the *poena* itself ought necessarily to be removed, for *poena* can never be inflicted except on account of *culpa* . . .".[133] Perhaps of greater relevance is a later comment in connection with I Corinthians 15:22 — "in Adam all die" — where we read: "Therefore in him (Adam) they also sinned and are held with him in a common *culpa*. For no one can merit the penalty of death in another unless with that other person and in him he has sin, which is the cause of death, in common with him. Nor is it sufficient to say that all die in Adam *efficienter* because we derive from Adam original sin, which is the cause of death. Because for the same reason we could be said to die in our parents . . . from whom we directly derive sin, and this the Scripture never says, but only from Adam. This is so because we were in Adam in a peculiar manner, not only as our seminal root but also as our representative head. So we are said to have sinned in him not only by reason of *efficiency*, as the cause by which sin is propagated to us, but also by reason of *demerit*, because his (Adam's) *culpa* has brought *reatus* upon us."[134]

[132] *Medulla Theologica*, Cap. XVII, §§2–4.
[133] *Op. cit.*, Loc. IX, Q. III, §VI.
[134] *Ibid.*, Loc. IX, Q. IX, §XVIII. It is also to be noted how other representative Reformed theologians declare in favour of this principle. David Pareus says: "Nos vero Adami culpam juste luimus. 1. Quia culpa sic est Adami, ut etiam sit nostra. Omnes enim in Adamo peccante peccauimus: Quia omnes in lumbis Adami fuimus. 2. Quia culpam Adami omnes natura trahimus, probamus, imitamur . . . . 3. Cum tota Adami natura sit rea, nos vero ex massa eius propagati simus, non possumus non etiam ipsi esse rei . . ." (*Corpus Doctrinae Christianae*, Pars I, Quaest. VII, Hanover, 1634, p. 46). Again, in reference to Romans 5:12, he says: "Sic tria in eo concurrerunt: culpa actualis, reatus legalis, pravitas naturalis: seu transgressio mandati, poena mortis, et corruptio naturae, quae

There can be little doubt, therefore, that the most representative of Reformed theologians were jealous to maintain that *reatus* and *poena* and, if we will, *reatus poenae*, always presuppose *culpa* and that, therefore, our involvement in the *reatus*, the obligation to penalty, of Adam's sin means that we were also involved in the *culpa* of his sin. To use Turretine's formula, "poena . . . nonnisi propter culpam potest infligi". If we have the *reatus* in common with Adam we must likewise have his *culpa*.

It was not only the Reformed theologians who maintained this correlativity of *culpa* and *poena*. The classic exponents of evangelical Lutheranism did likewise, and the similarity in mode of statement is apparent. David Hollaz can say: "The first sin of Adam, inasmuch as he is regarded as the common parent, head, root, and representative of the whole human race is truly and by the just judgment of God imputed to all

fuit amissio imaginis Dei . . . . An ullo horum posteritas mansit immunis, sed omnia simul ad posteros introierunt non una via, sed triplici: Participatione culpae, imputatione reatus, propagatione naturalis pravitatis. *Participatione culpae*, quia omnes posteri seminali ratione fuerunt in lumbis Adami. Ibi omnes in Adamo peccante peccaverunt . . . . *Imputatione reatus*, quia primus homo ita stabat in gratia, ut si peccaret, non ipse solus, sed tota posteritas ea excideret, reaque cum ipso fieret aeternae mortis . . . . Atque hoc est, quod primum Adae peccatum nobis imputari dicitur. *Naturali* denique *propagatione* seu generatione horribilis naturae deformitas cum tristi reatu in omnes posteros sese diffudit" (*In Divinam ad Romanos Epistolam Commentarius*, p. 119). Later on in this commentary, in referring to the first sin of Adam, Pareus says: "Non (inquit) ita fuit unius, quin et omnium fuit. In uno omnes illud admiserunt: alioqui mors in omnes transire non potuisset. Qui enim non peccant, hoc est, nulla culpa et reatu tenentur, ut Sancti Angeli: in eos mors nil iuris habet. Quia vero mors in omnes transiit omnes igitur peccaverunt, hoc est, culpa et reatu tenentur" (*ibid.*, p. 120). *Cf.*, also, B. de Moor: *Commentarius Perpetuus in Johannis Markii Compendium Theologiae Christianae*, (Leyden, 1765), Pars III, pp. 254 f.; William Bucanus: *Institutions of Christian Religion* (E. T., London, 1606), pp. 158–161; Benedict Pictet: *Theologia Christiana* (London, 1820), p. 147. Robert W. Landis in *The Doctrine of Original Sin as Received and Taught by the Churches of the Reformation Stated and Defended* (Richmond, 1884) deals at great length with this question and others related to it. This lengthy monograph is devoted to a large extent to criticism of Dr. Hodge's position, and particularly of what Landis calls the gratuitous imputation of Adam's sin to the race, a position which he considers to be that of Hodge.

his posterity for *culpa* and *poena*".[135] And Quenstedt says to
much the same effect: "For in the sin of the first man there
concur: 1. actual *culpa*, 2. legal *reatus*, 3. natural pravity.
All of these entered into the world at the same time, and into
all Adam's posterity. For we are involved (1) in participation
of the actual *culpa*, inasmuch as we all sinned in Adam,
(2) in the imputation of the legal *reatus*, for the first man
stood and fell as head . . ., and (3) by propagation of natural
pravity, because it spreads to all men through natural conception."[136]

We thus find that Reformed and Lutheran theologians did
not conceive of the *reatus* of Adam's sin as imputed to posterity
apart from the *culpa* of the same sin. And this is simply to
say that the relation of posterity to the sin of Adam could
not be construed or defined merely in terms of the obligation
to satisfy justice (*reatus poenae*) but must also include, as
the antecedent and ground of that *reatus*, involvement in the
culpa of Adam's transgression. Hence when Dr. Hodge says
that the imputation of the guilt of Adam's sin to posterity
does not mean the imputation of "criminality" or "demerit"
but only of "the judicial obligation to satisfy justice", we
discover what we are compelled to regard as a divergence
from the older Reformed theologians in respect of a principle
which they esteemed basic in the construction of the doctrine
of our relation to the first sin of Adam. It is just precisely
the involvement of posterity in the *culpa* of Adam's sin that
Hodge is jealous to deny, when these other theologians were
insistent that *poena* and *culpa* are inseparable and that *reatus*
arises from *culpa* and leads to *poena*. And it would appear
that the difficulty which we found with Dr. Hodge's position

[135] *Examen Theologicum Acromaticum*, "Theologia", Pars II, Cap. III,
Quaest. X (Leipzig, 1763, p. 513).

[136] *Theologia Didactico-Polemica* (Leipzig, 1715), Pars II, col. 914. The
similarity of Quenstedt's terminology to that of Pareus, as quoted above,
is quite apparent. *Cf.*, also, L. Hütterus: *Compendium Theologicum* as
revised by G. Cundisius (Jena, 1652), p. 573; J. Gerhard: *Loci Theologici*,
Loc. IX, Cap. III, §53 where the language is not the same as in the preceding but points in the same direction; Heinrich Schmid: *The Doctrinal
Theology of the Evangelical Lutheran Church* (E. T., Philadelphia, 1889),
pp. 247 ff.; Francis Pieper: *Christian Dogmatics* (Saint Louis, 1950), vol. I,
pp. 538 ff.

from the standpoint of exegesis, specifically the exegesis of Romans 5:12, 19, lies close to this divergence on Hodge's part from the formulation of other Reformed theologians. In other words, it may be that the shortcoming which adheres to Hodge's position in respect of exegesis is the shortcoming which the other Reformed theologians sought to avoid by the very insistence which we have discussed. It can at least be said that if posterity are regarded as involved in the *culpa* of Adam's sin, then we have an additional factor in terms ot which to interpret "all sinned" and were "constituted sinners"

To return to the question at issue, namely, the definition of that which is imputed to posterity or, in other words, the import of "all sinned" and "the many were constituted sinners" (Rom. 5:12, 19), it appears to the present writer illegitimate to restrict the imputation to "the judicial obligation to satisfy justice" or to what has often been called *reatus poenae*. The basic reason for this judgment has been indicated already. In the crucial passage (Rom. 5:12–19) Paul not only speaks of the wages of sin as penetrating to all, not only of the judicial condemnation as coming upon all, but also of all as implicated in the sin of Adam with the result that they became sinners. There is likewise the theological consideration to which the Reformed theologians were sensitive that to impute penal liability without the imputation of that to which the penal liability is due is faced with a juridical objection. Although it is not ours to solve all mysteries and by no means ours to call in question the government of God in inflicting the whole race with the penal consequences of Adam's own sin, yet we have no need or right to complicate the mystery by making the kind of disjunction which the notion of the mere imputation of judicial liability entails. The Scripture does not make this disjunction and we may not lay upon our theological formulation a liability which the Scripture itself does not warrant and from which its express statements steer us away.

It is fully to be admitted that the doctrine of our involvement in the one trespass of Adam is one that has to be properly guarded against misconstruction and we may not lay it open to interpretations which conflict with other biblical principles.

When we say that we are involved in the trespass of Adam and that it is reckoned to us as our sin, we must insist as jealously as did Hodge and other theologians that we, the members of posterity, did not personally and voluntarily as individuals eat of the forbidden fruit. And neither are we to posit any such notion as the *transfer* from Adam to us of the moral character involved in his trespass. At least we must not regard any such postulate as indispensable to the proposition that Adam's trespass is also ours in its character as sin. On the other hand, we must not so attenuate our involvement that what is conceived of as ours is merely the judicial liability or some other consequence of sin. Out of deference to the biblical teaching we shall have to recognize and make allowance for a real involvement on our part in Adam's sin that is not to be construed as actual, voluntary participation or the *transfer* of moral character, on the one hand, and yet is not to be reduced to the level of judicial liability, on the other. We must insist on the involvement of posterity in Adam's sin in a way that will place this involvement in the category of sin and yet maintain that it was Adam's trespass in a manner that is not ours. In the language of theology we must try to do justice to both considerations, that, in respect of posterity, Adam's trespass was both *peccatum alienum* and *peccatum proprium.*

In pursuing this inquiry it should be understood that we are doing so on the express assumption of the immediate imputation to posterity of Adam's sin, and the only question now is: what is entailed in that imputation so as to make it truly an imputation of *sin*?

The expression which Paul uses, "constituted sinners", is parallel and antithetical to the other expression in the apodosis of Romans 5:19, namely, "constituted righteous". The latter expression plainly refers to an action which falls within the ambit of justification. This is the theme with which Paul is dealing in this part of the epistle and to interpret "constituted righteous" in terms diverse from "the righteousness of God" (Rom. 1:17; 3:21, 22) brought to bear upon us unto justification, "the free gift from many trespasses unto justification" (Rom. 5:16), "the free gift of righteousness" (Rom. 5:17), "the one righteous act . . . unto justification of life" (Rom.

5:18), and the grace that reigns "through righteousness unto eternal life" (Rom. 5:21) would be a travesty of exegesis. It is a legitimate question whether the constitutive act of Romans 5:19 is the logical antecedent of the justifying act, or is embraced in the justifying act itself. But this question does not affect the fact that "constituted righteous" must derive its character from the nature of justification. Now, if anything is apparent from Scripture usage and from the teaching of Paul in particular, it is that justification is forensic — it has reference to a judicial sentence. It is no more subjectively operative in its import than is condemnation. Hence "constituted righteous" must have forensic import — it has reference to an act of God which contemplates forensic relationship, the relationship which a person is conceived of as sustaining to law and justice. Since it is obviously an act of God which is concerned with a radical change of relationship, it must mean that God constitutes a new judicial relation to himself in virtue of which the person may be declared to be righteous in his sight. And since it is by "the obedience of the one" that this relationship is constituted, there can be but one conclusion, that by an act of grace the obedience of Christ is brought to bear upon the person concerned in such a way that the judgment registered with respect to that person is the judgment which the obedience of Christ elicits and demands. To put it otherwise, the person is given property in the obedience of Christ with the result that his judicial status is that belonging to the obedience in which he has come to have property; this is the act of grace involved in being "constituted righteous".

The parallel antithesis, "constituted sinners", will have to be interpreted along similar lines. In relation to the precise inquiry being conducted it cannot be reduced to lower terms than those which we find, antithetically, in "constituted righteous". And perhaps the most relevant way of stating the case by way of parallel is that posterity came to have property in Adam's disobedience with the result that their judicial status is that belonging to the disobedience in which they have property. The disobedience of Adam is brought to bear upon posterity in such a way that the judgment registered upon them is the judgment which the disobedience of Adam elicits and demands. If we may speak in terms of imputation, there is as truly an imputation of the disobedience of Adam as there is of the obedience of Christ. As the latter imputation is not that of the benefit accruing but that the benefit accruing follows upon the imputation, so the former must not be conceived of as the liability entailed but the liability as flowing from the imputation. It is within the sphere of the forensic that the imputation takes place, but the imputation must not be defined in any other terms than those of disobedience and obedience. Viewed from the standpoint of personal, voluntary action the disobedience in the one case is that of Adam and the obedience is that of Christ. But the effect of the "constituting" act is that others, not personally and voluntarily engaged, come to have property, indeed propriety, in the personal, voluntary performance of another. It is both *alienum* and *proprium*, and neither aspect must be stressed to the exclusion of the other.

When we take account of what occurs in the realm of grace and appreciate the reality of the believer's property in the righteousness of Christ and the centrality of this truth in the gospel of grace, it is not only feasible but it is incu.nbent upon us to reckon with a parallel property in the sin of Adam. It is totally indefensible to exclude the possibility of a divine judgment and government by which the sin of Adam is reckoned to be as really and properly ours as is the righteousness of Christ in justification. And that this is actually the case is the witness of Scripture. It may be that this is the limit of revelation to us respecting the involvement of posterity in the one trespass of Adam. But even should this be the case it is sufficient to establish the reality of our property in nothing less than his sin, and, with the proper qualifications already stated, there does not appear to be any good reason why this property should not be called, as some of the older theologians stated, participation in the *culpa* of his transgression.

It may not be without warrant, however, to pursue the question still further. In any case theologians of the Reformed family have done so and it may not be useless to conduct this pursuit.[137] The terms "constituted righteous" (Rom. 5:19) must be interpreted, as has been shown, within the ambit of justification and therefore forensically. We may not, however, overlook the fact that it is in union with Christ that this constitutive action takes place. It is in virtue of union with Christ that believers come to have property in Christ's righteousness unto their justification. And though nothing must be pleaded to tone down the forensic nature of justification, yet with equal emphasis the virtue emanating from union with Christ must not be restricted to justification. All the grace bestowed upon believers finds it ground or basis in union with Christ in his death and resurrection. The subjective renewal which is concomitant with justification springs from this union, for it is in virtue of solidarity with Christ in his death and resurrection that the regenerative operations of the Holy Spirit take place in the believer, whether regeneration is logically prior to justification, as some maintain, or logically posterior, as others hold. In this way regeneration, though wrought by the agency of the Holy Spirit, stems from solidarity with Christ in his once-for-all accomplishment. If we follow this direction of thought and apply it to our union with Adam we may properly find that although "constituted sinners" (Rom. 5:19) cannot be made to express any more than the forensic relation to Adam's sin, yet solidarity with Adam implies more by way of involvement in sin than that expressed in forensic terms. We may not try to trace parallels in every detail; in the operations of redemptive grace there are factors which far transcend the operations of judgment in our relation to Adam's sin, as Paul observes in Romans 5:12–19. But a parallel to this extent is surely not without warrant, that as representative solidarity with Christ in his obedience unto death and in his resurrection secures and insures subjective renewal in regeneration, so representative solidarity with Adam in his sin involved for posterity their subjective depravity as well as the forensic judgment of their being "constituted sinners". In this way a basis may be laid for a better understanding of the relation which the infliction

---

[137] Cf. Thomas Goodwin: Works (Edinburgh, 1865), vol. X, pp. 47–55; Jonathan Edwards: Works (New York, 1855), vol. II, pp. 481–495.

of posterity with depravity sustains to the one trespass of Adam. And depravity may not be conceived of so much as a penal infliction arising from the imputation of Adam's sin but as an implicate of solidarity with Adam in his sin. Pravity is thus itself a constituent element of identification with Adam in his trespass, and we can no more be exempted from the pravity which Adam's trespass involved than we can be relieved of the forensic judgment which passed upon it. It may contribute to elucidation and support of this position if we set forth the following theses.

(1) The members of posterity cannot be conceived of as existing when Adam trespassed. To posit any such supposition is to contradict the meaning of conception and generation as the divinely constituted means for the origin of all members of the race except the first pair. Yet all the members of the race were contemplated by God as destined to exist; they were foreordained to be and the certainty of their existence was thus guaranteed. It is important in this connection to bear in mind that as *thus contemplated* by God they were contemplated no otherwise than as members of the race in solidaric union with Adam and therefore as having sinned in him. In other words, they are not conceived of in the mind and purpose of God except as one with Adam; they are not contemplated as potentially but as actually one with Adam in his sin. And this proposition is basic to all further thought on the question.

(2) All the members of the race come to exist actually by the act or process of generation; this is the divinely constituted means whereby God's foreordained design comes to effect in the course of history. It is a capital mistake to interpose the question: when does each member of the race *become* actually sinful? For the truth is that each person never exists as other than sinful. He is eternally contemplated by God as sinful by reason of the solidarity with Adam, and, whenever the person comes to be *actually*, he comes to be as sinful. Sinfulness is correlative with his beginning to be as an individual in his mother's womb. If, for the moment, we speak of the soul as the seat of personality, it runs counter to all the implications of our solidarity with Adam to think of the soul as ever existing or as conceived by God to exist as a pure

entity undefiled by sin. The soul or, to speak more properly, the person never exists apart from the sin of Adam's transgression.

(3) If we ask the question: when is the sin of Adam imputed? the answer is apparent. The imputation is correlative with the beginning to be. This is only another way of saying what was stated in the preceding paragraph. Sin is intertwined with our very existence in view of Adamic solidarity.

(4) When we attempt to define this involvement that is correlative with our origin as individuals, we cannot say less than that we are reckoned as having sinned in Adam. It must be fully appreciated that theologians who define imputation in terms of the obligation to punishment are at the same time sustained and emphatic in the use of such formulae as "we sinned in Adam", "we are reckoned as having sinned in Adam", "the sin of Adam is imputed to us". And this is evidence that, although they are virtually deserting this ground when they define sin in terms merely of *reatus poenae*, they are yet unable to abandon the formulae which reflect the biblical teaching and which are demanded in their true and proper import if the implications of our solidarity with Adam are to be rightly assessed. It would appear that the reason why Dr. Hodge, for example, can temporarily waive the proper import of these formulae and adopt a definition that is on lower ground is that he had not been ready to entertain the implications which a valid use of these formulae involved.

(5) The sin of Adam was what all sin is, transgression of the law of God. As such it was pravity and perversity; it was *culpa* without mitigation. It is impossible to think of his trespass apart from these characterisations. When sin is predicated of him it would be an abstraction to posit such predication apart from these characterising conditions. Likewise, when we think of the solidarity of the race with Adam in his sin, is it not an abstraction to think of posterity's involvement apart from these same characterisations? If we may not make this abstraction it means that the solidarity of the race with Adam's trespass requires us to infer that the pravity and perversity of sin are entailed for posterity in their iden-

tification with the original trespass. This is simply to say that when each member of the race comes to exist he exists, from the inception of his being, as depraved with that perversity which his solidaric identification with the sin of Adam involves.

If this analysis is correct, then the question of the relation of depravity to the imputation of the trespass of Adam is placed in a different perspective from that frequently supposed. The representation usually made by those maintaining immediate imputation is that the infliction of the race with depravity is the penal consequence of the imputation of Adam's sin. It is not so certain, however, that this is the most accurate analysis or that it rests upon a biblical basis. On the foregoing construction the case would be that the infliction with depravity is involved in the imputation of Adam's sin; our involvement in and identification with the sin of Adam carries with it as a necessary ingredient the pravity or perversity apart from which sin does not exist. In other words, the imputation of Adam's sin carries with it, not merely as consequence but as implicate, the depravity with which all the members of the race begin their existence as distinct individuals. The imputation is not thus conceived of as something causally antecedent to the depravity but as that which includes depravity as an element.

Furthermore, the relation of depravity to natural generation may also have to be formulated in a different fashion. It may not be strictly accurate to say that we become depraved by natural generation. It is true that *in* the act of generation we become depraved. This is true because it is by generation that we come to be as distinct persons. In this sense it would not be improper to say that we become depraved by natural generation. But natural generation is not the reason why we are conceived in sin. It is not an adequate explanation of our depravity to say that by the law of generation like begets like and since Adam became depraved it was inevitable that he should beget children in the same depraved condition. It is necessary, of course, to take account of this factor. But the *reason* why we are naturally generated in sin is that, whenever we begin to be, we begin to be as sinful because of our solidarity with Adam in his sin. Thus the relation of

natural generation to depravity is that by the former we
begin to be and having begun to be we are necessarily sinful
by reason of our involvement in Adam's sin. Natural generation we may speak of, if we will, as the means of conveying
depravity, but, strictly, natural generation is the means
whereby we come to be and depravity is the correlate of our
having come to be. We may not think that the most relevant
biblical statements provide us with a different construction.
"In sin did my mother conceive me" (Psalm 51:5), "that
which is born of the flesh is flesh" (John 3:6), and "by nature
children of wrath, even as others" (Eph. 2:3) point to the
fact that we are conceived and born corrupt. But these texts
do not go further than to establish the fact that we are
depraved from our mother's womb and that natural generation
inevitably produces corrupt human nature.

Objections to this construction of the relation of depravity
to the imputation of Adam's sin are easily anticipated.
Perhaps the most plausible is that the parallel between the
imputation of Adam's sin to us and the imputation of our
sins to Christ breaks down if this analysis is correct. For on
no account may we give quarter to the suggestion or lend
any support to it that in the imputation of our sins to Christ
in his vicarious sin-bearing there was any such involvement
as infliction with the pravity of sin. Our Lord was holy,
harmless, undefiled, and separate from sinners; he was without
spot and blameless and no pravity touched his soul. This is
an axiom of Christian belief and to compromise here is to
abandon Christianity. But to urge this as an objection to the
formulation in question is quite invalid. There are several
observations.

(1) The imputation of Adam's sin to posterity carries with
it *in any event* the infliction of the race with depravity.
Whether we conceive of this depravity as implicate of the
imputation or as penal consequence, it is an inevitable result.
There was no pravity resulting for our Lord from his vicarious
sin-bearing. Since there is this radical and patent difference,
the question at issue is not affected if we conceive of the
depravity that comes upon posterity as something entailed
in the imputation of Adam's sin. The implications of imputation in the respective cases are radically different in respect

of the pravity in connection with which the objection is raised.
Hence the objection has no validity.

(2) The vicarious sin-bearing of Christ and the imputation
which it presupposes are in a unique category. We must
not allow this uniqueness to be prejudiced by drawing the
parallel to the imputation of Adam's sin in such close terms
that we virtually obliterate the differences. These differences
are so basic that to discover a radical differentiation in this
matter of pravity would exemplify the unparalleled features
of Christ's vicarious sin-bearing.

(3) In interpreting the sin-bearing of Christ we have too
limited a conception of its involvements for him if we view it
in terms merely of *penal* satisfaction. Christ indeed bore the
penalty of the sins of his people. But the tendency to restrict
his sin-bearing to the bare notion of penalty impoverishes our
appreciation of what his vicarious sacrifice demanded and
entailed. Suffice it to be reminded that the Scriptures do not
describe his undertaking as consisting only in the endurance
of our penalty; "he bore our *sins*". "The Lord hath laid
upon him the iniquity of us all." He stood in the closest
relation to our *sins* that it was possible for him to sustain
without becoming himself defiled thereby, and this is the
mystery of humiliation, of grace, and of love that eternity
will not exhaust. This perspective with respect to Christ's
vicarious sin-bearing is parallel in this locus of doctrine to
the other contention in connection with the imputation of
Adam's sin, namely, that the latter is not to be construed as
consisting simply in *reatus poenae*. A deeper appreciation of
the meaning of Christ's sin-bearing and of the imputation it
involved points to a more inclusive concept of what is entailed
in the imputation of Adam's sin.

(4) On the point of the objection it must not be overlooked
that the precise expressions used in Scripture with reference
to the solidarity of the race in Adam's sin are not paralleled
in connection with Christ's sin-bearing. With reference to
posterity we read that "all sinned" and "the many were
constituted sinners". But, though Christ is said to have been
"made sin for us" (II Cor. 5:21), to have been "made a curse"
(Gal. 3:13), to have borne our sins (I Pet. 2:24), to have been
sent "in the likeness of sinful flesh and for sin" (Rom. 8:3),

yet we do not read that he sinned or was constituted a sinner. There is in this discrimination an index to the difference that must be posited between imputation as it applies to Adam's sin and as it applies to Christ's sin-bearing. To find differentiation, as it pertains to pravity, in the precise manner formulated above is not only consonant with the difference but exemplifies the same in a way that is most appropriate.

It may be that thought on this question of our relation to the sin of Adam has been given too restricted a direction by excessive concentration on the notion of imputation. If we keep in view what lies at the basis of imputation, namely, union or solidarity with Adam and therefore solidarity with Adam in his trespass, we are given a concept that provides for and points in the direction of a more inclusive definition of what is involved for posterity in the imputation of Adam's sin.

If the involvement of posterity in the first sin of Adam is recognised to carry with it as implicate or ingredient the pravity which Adam's trespass implied, this construction performs a threefold service. First, it provides us with a line of thought which imparts to the idea of the sin of all in the sin of Adam an import that measures up to the definition of sin. The sin of posterity is not that of mere *reatus* abstracted from the only proper basis of *reatus*, namely, sin itself. Secondly, it brings the doctrine of the immediate imputation of Adam's sin to its logical rights because this construction finds in the depravity with which posterity is inflicted the direct implicate of solidarity with Adam's sin — pravity is itself an ingredient of the solidaric sin. And, thirdly, it vindicates the analysis which was characteristic of both Reformed and Lutheran theologians that *reatus poenae* presupposes *culpa*. On the foregoing analysis *culpa* is clearly exhibited in solidaric pravity.

DATE DUE

MAR 0 1 1983	MAR 2 2 1988	OCT 0 7 2005	
APR 0 5 1983	APR 2 6 1988	DEC 2 3 2009	
MAY 0 3 1983	NOV 8	SEP 2 8 2011	
JUN 5 '84	MAR 2 3 1992		
MAY 3 0 '85	NOV 1 1994	DEC 2 3 2011	
JUN 1 1 '85	MAY 0 6 1996	NOV 2 0 2013	
APR 1 1986	NOV 1 9 1996	FEB 2 3 2014	
MAY 1 9 1987	OCT 0 5 1999		
DEC 1 1987	NOV 0 2 1999		
JAN 7 2 1988	Jan 06	JAN 2 3 1988	
MAR 0 4 1992			